HOLISTIC THERAPY FOR PEOPLE WITH DISSOCIATIVE IDENTITY DISORDER

HOLISTIC THERAPY FOR PEOPLE WITH DISSOCIATIVE IDENTITY DISORDER

Edited by
Patricia Frankish and Valerie Sinason

KARNAC

First published in 2017 by
Karnac Books Ltd
118 Finchley Road
London NW3 5HT

British Library Cataloguing in Publication Data

A C.I.P. for this book is available from the British Library

ISBN-13: 978-1-78220-563-0

Typeset by Medlar Publishing Solutions Pvt Ltd, India

www.karnacbooks.com

CONTENTS

ACKNOWLEDGEMENTS

Many people have contributed to this book and the service described. We, as editors, are extremely grateful to them. We specially want to mention Kelly Calpin, Sharron Jones, Nicki Donkin, Amanda Brock, Carrie-Anne Smith, Cathy Gibbs, Natalie Cross, Carole Richardson, and all those brave people who continue to live with DID.

Patricia Frankish is a clinical psychologist and psychotherapist with many years of experience in the field of disability. Her doctoral study established a method for measuring emotional developmental stages in people who had suffered trauma and consequent interference in the developmental process. She is from Lincolnshire and after working in a range of settings and spending six years in North Yorkshire and Teesside, she has settled back in Lincolnshire with her own business in partnership with her daughter. They specialise in providing services for people with complex needs, using the model that Pat has developed. They offer direct support, training, and therapy, either as a package or one component. For those who need it they also provide accommodation. Pat has been President of the British Psychological Society, was a founding member of the Institute of Psychotherapy and Disability, and is an active member of her local Church and community.

Valerie Sinason is a poet, writer, child psychotherapist and adult psychoanalyst. She is Founder Director of the Clinic for Dissociative Studies and President of the Institute for Psychotherapy and Disability. She is an Honorary Consultant Psychotherapist at the University of Cape Town Child Guidance Clinic and Chair of Trustees of the First People

Centre, New Bethesda, South Africa. She is a Patron of Dorset Action on Abuse (DAA), editor of *Trauma Dissociation and Multiplicity* and co-editor of *Psychoanalytic Psychotherapy after Child abuse*. She has published numerous articles and books, including two poetry collections. Valerie Sinason was awarded a Lifetime Achievement Award from the ISSTD (International Society for the Study of Trauma and Dissociation) in April 2016.

INTRODUCTION

It was parents' evening at a school for children with mental health and disability problems. There had been concern for a nine-year-old girl, Brenda (not her real name), a wheelchair user, who had suddenly become very volatile, shouting at staff one moment and crying the next. Her drawings were full of girls in wheelchairs racing round a huge bedroom with smiles on their faces. The class teacher was very relieved that Brenda's mother, unusually, had come to the evening and had asked the school therapist to talk to her. The woman was white-faced, grimacing with pain, and tears were falling down her face. She was being evicted from the private flat she lived in with her daughter. Her physically abusive partner had suggested she prostitute herself to provide them with better housing. She had been offered a small unsuitable place with no adequate wheelchair room. It was hard for her to take in the fact that her daughter was being offered once-weekly therapy in school; that the class teacher had wondered about what room Brenda had to move about the flat in her wheelchair. "Her having room to move? What about me? What about us? What about the rest of the time when there is no therapy? What about evenings? What about weekends? What about my partner?"

Teachers have long recognised that the most common time for a child to disclose abuse and other trauma is 4 pm on a Friday afternoon, just as everyone is leaving for the weekend. After hours is a painful time for children and adults who do not have an outside or inside sense or reality of safety and security. Whilst lucky children look forward to the break that a weekend can provide, others experience it as a time of danger, terror, relentless punishment and abuse, or loneliness. Unsupported parents, with problems of their own or with children with problems, can find the periods of no school equally difficult.

As a trainee teacher and then a psychotherapist within schools for children with disabilities or mental health problems, I was concerned for both of these groups. I watched as small people left for a weekend with big people many of the staff were frightened of. Additionally, I would be aware of the lack of support for vulnerable parents in weekend and holiday periods, which in turn exacerbated the risks to the children.

The lack of safe and containing evening and weekend resources for vulnerable children and adults is serious across all client groups. With regard to those with intellectual disabilities and mental health problems, my father, the late Professor Stanley Segal OBE, used to add on evening classes in his schools for children with intellectual disabilities. He wanted to help support the parents by including them under the containing school umbrella. As a child I would be impressed by his concern at the depleted lives his charges had when they left the school environment, and, more particularly, when they left the school. He and my mother would take my brother and I to Seaford, East Sussex, for our yearly holiday where they ran a branch of the Children's Country Holiday Fund. From their own experience of childhood deprivation (despite love) they wanted to make sure others had an experience of a residential holiday.

It was no surprise in 1967 when he and my mother left London so he could be principal of a residential community for people with intellectual disabilities. Ravenswood Village brought him enormous relief. He was able to enrich the lives of children and adults on a twenty-four-hour daily cycle. Parents couldn't be expected to provide the same level of stimulation for their adult children with disabilities, he insisted.

Historically, learning disability in itself precluded someone from a talking therapy (Sinason, 1994, 2002) and the Department of Health (DH) awareness of extra vulnerability to abuse in this population was hard for society to accept (McQueen, Kennedy, Itzin, Sinason, & Maxted, 2008).

When first encountering children and adults with a dissociative identity disorder (DID) in the 1990s, including those with learning disabilities, it is not surprising that one of the first concerns was what happened to them in the rest of the week outside the one, two, three, or four hours of therapy. Were they emotionally, physically, and sexually safe? Were they spiritually safe? Did they have any sense of "home" that nurtured them?

While this condition crosses all social classes, levels of ability and disability, ethnic groups, and belief systems, a theme of unsafeness persists. As Sachs and Galton (2008) have clarified, DID is par excellence a forensic condition in that it is largely created by a crime, whether of commission or omission, against a child. Ninety per cent of patients meeting the DSM-5 (APA, 2013) criteria for DID report a history of sexual and physical abuse (Fonagy & Target, 1995).

DID, formerly known as multiple personality disorder, is a survival mechanism in the face of a disorganised attachment and, often, abuse in early childhood by an attachment figure. Where it is not safe for a child to see and comprehend her unsafeness, a dissociation of memory and ongoing living is necessary to preserve the idea of a safe-enough life. By dissociating from and splitting off terrifying images of a caregiver, the child is able to keep a positive attachment image in order to survive.

Many children and adults who face abuse at the hands of an attachment figure do not develop DID. It requires a disorganised attachment in addition to abuse and trauma. A nineteen-year follow-up of infants with a disorganised attachment revealed a tendency to develop dissociative disorders (Ogawa, Stroufe, Weinfield, Carlson, & Egeland, 1997).

Attachment theory, first researched by Bowlby (1969), is a child of psychoanalysis and ethology. It shows that all mammals require attachment for survival. In the face of danger the young mammal seeks out an attachment figure for proximity and safety. Where there is a secure attachment the parent or caregiver provides a containing response that allows reflection and resilience.

Disorganised attachment was delineated (Main & Hesse, 1990) as a third and most serious form of insecure attachment. This is often seen as coming from an experience of "fear without solution" in which the caregiver is perceived as frightened or frightening. Liotti (1995) has shown that such parents might have their own unresolved history of loss and maltreatment. This highlights the importance of intervention at all stages of the lifecycle to avoid generational transmission of trauma.

Whilst attachment theory has scientifically validated the development of and need for dissociative defences, an urban myth, largely propagated by a small number of "false memory" groups, that DID is a "controversial" diagnosis, has taken hold of some sections of the British media and found its way into some professional groups.

As the published findings (McQueen, Kennedy, Itzin, Sinason, & Maxted, 2008) of Professor Catherine Itzin's DH-funded research on therapy after abuse comment: "Although, historically, there has been debate over the existence and true prevalence of dissociative identity disorder, it is a valid diagnostic entity that can be reliably diagnosed." (Gabbard, 2005)

DSM-5 definition of DID

- Two or more distinct personality states/alters are present, and each must have its own way of being.
- Amnesia is a requirement, but the DSM-5 has altered the wording to: "Recurrent gaps in the recall of everyday events, important personal information, and/or traumatic events that are inconsistent with ordinary forgetting".
- An individual must be distressed by the disorder or have an impaired ability to function in a major area of life as a result. This is described as follows: "The symptoms cause clinically significant distress or impairment in social, occupational, or other important areas of functioning".
- Normal cultural or religious practice is excluded, and fantasy play in children is excluded. The disturbance is not a normal part of a broadly accepted cultural or religious practice.
- DID cannot be diagnosed if symptoms are attributable to substance use or other medical conditions. "The symptoms are not attributable to the physiological effects of a substance (e.g., blackouts or chaotic behavior during alcohol intoxication) or another medical condition (e.g., complex partial seizures)".

Specialist multidisciplinary assessments for DID include therapeutic interview, psychiatric assessment, and psychological structured clinical interview for DSM-IV dissociative disorders (SCID-D) assessment. The SCID-D was developed by Marlene Steinberg MD as a result of her research at Yale University. Most specialist clinics, such as the Pottergate Centre and the Clinic for Dissociative Studies, use these multidisciplinary tools. Further input can include memory research, which highlights the level of amnesia and differentiates from subjective or objective memory (Morton, 2012).

Multiple research now exists on the scientific reality of DID from brain scan and physiology and fantasy proneness. Indeed, key researchers Nijenhuis and Reinders (2012) have now empirically shown that fantasy proneness is not a problem in DID.

However, having a diagnosis that DID exists does not answer whether it is stable or volatile (Sachs, 2014), whether ordinary living function is dramatically damaged or not. Some individuals are extremely lucky in the loving support they have. We are focusing here on those for whom having to "switch" mental states in order to survive entails increasing vulnerability that can affect livelihood, relationships, and ongoing stability. Whilst some people with DID achieve a stable level of functioning in which the main personality knows how to avoid triggers, those who come to clinical attention often have their lives and livelihoods and families put at risk by inconsistent, volatile faces they present to the outside world where there is no understanding of their condition.

Indeed, some of the first patients with DID that I knowingly encountered in the early 1990s presented with a need for both intensive psychotherapy and supportive living aid. (As with all supposedly "new" topics, the clinician realises too late what they failed to recognise earlier!)

Unfortunately, in the UK, there are very few psychodynamic residential communities such as Arbours, which can provide holistic containment with psychodynamic understanding. Indeed, for many of those adults we encounter in clinical work, a psychiatric hospital is rarely the adequate container. The lack of psychodynamic understanding and lack of training in DID can mean that patients feel more damaged through the experience even if they are kept physically safe from outside abusers.

Even at the psychodynamic end of residential containment there can be a problem where there is inadequate experience of DID as libertarian communities allow patients to leave at night of their own volition (without being able to assess the danger of particular personalities overriding the rest of the system by leaving).

This means that all over the UK there are people with DID, children and adults, and their carers/families/teams looking for suitable wrap-around virtual or real therapeutic communities. Whilst, at times, the Clinic for Dissociative Studies, as a specialist independent provider, has tried to create a bespoke virtual therapeutic community this is hard to achieve and a real, face-to-face, twenty-four-hour presence is required.

Dr Pat Frankish, a leading disability therapy pioneer and a former president of the British Psychological Society (BPS) has for many years established a unique therapeutic residential plan. She and her team create a bespoke residential therapeutic care plan around individual patients with disabilities. This includes training for support staff, psychologists, and disability psychotherapists. As her staff encountered more and more cases of people with DID requiring residential care (with or without an intellectual disability) they all realised that the Frankish model could be provided as a template to other hospitals and clinics rather like Dr Sandra Bloom's Sanctuary model which at first was housed in one particular hospital but has now been widely applied.

Dr Frankish and her team have for many years wished to publish in more detail the successful outcomes of their work and training. Indeed, it took until 2015 for the first major disability book to appear (Frankish, 2015). Having witnessed over years the development of the residential programmes, the successful accreditation of the first disability therapy training in the UK, and the theoretical structures that have underpinned this work, I and others have encouraged Dr Frankish and her committed teams to write further on how their model applies to dissociative disorders for adults with or without an intellectual disability.

As with several recent books on DID (Bowlby & Briggs, 2014; Hoffman, 2015; Miller, 2012; Sinason, 2002, 2012; Van der Merwe & Sinason, 2016) there has been a clinical, social, and ethical dilemma in how to most safely express the most crucial voice—the voice of the survivor.

The number of survivors of sexual abuse who are willing to go to the police remains low, and with DID even more so. The number of cases that even get to court is a small fraction of estimated abuse and the number that achieve resolution in the courts is even smaller. Against that we have the national and international increase in awareness of the long-term damage to physical and mental health that comes from untreated trauma and the most likely diagnoses that follow.

The whole of human society depends on relating and trusting that the narrative of those around us is largely accurate. We do not speak of "alleged" bed wetters or "alleged" burglars. When a patient comes to see us a neutral position is not one of sceptical disbelief or unthinking belief. We are all aware that distortion occurs in human narratives and no one who wasn't there can exactly say what has happened or not happened to another. However, trauma therapy understands that the mental distress a patient presents with has origins in the outside world as well as the internal representation. Indeed, the Bowlby Centre code of values includes in its five core statements the following three that deal with reality:

- Mental distress has its origin in failed or inadequate attachment relationships in early life and is best treated in the context of a long-term human relationship.
- Attachment relationships are shaped in the real world and impacted upon by poverty, discrimination, and social inequality—the impact of the social world will be part of the therapy.
- Those who have been silenced about their experiences and survival strategies must have their reality acknowledged and not pathologised.

As a survivor clearly writes:

> What I need is that you believe that what I tell you is my truth; that my recollections of extreme cruelty are not beyond the realms of belief. To walk beside me you must believe human beings are capable of inflicting the kind of abuse and horror that I remember. Demonstrating you do is the key of belief you can give without compromising therapeutic neutrality. (IS, 2006, p. 11)

The moment one kind of abuse is deemed impossible to happen we lose a whole group of children and adults to appalling practices. Whether, historically, it was not deemed possible that a religious leader could behave like this, or a mother, or a sibling, or a group, or an MP or a minister, we have a different cut-off now—ritualistic abuse of white, middle-class children (as opposed to black, working-class ones), or military mind control procedures. Holding in mind what humans can and do inflict on each other across the world is crucial.

This is even more important when a significant percentage of clinical narratives include abuse carried out under the aegis or purported aegis of a belief system. Whether the abusers believe in the supposedly religious ideas they have frightened their victims with, or are only using religion as a means of adding to fear, we may never know. However, the important issue is that where the survivors believe what they have been told, it has become internalised in them. Raising issues of spiritual abuse within a largely secular society is a more problematic issue. The NSPCC (Edwards, 2005) has published guidance on abuse linked to spirit possession (Stobart, 2006) including details of the tortures children describe—largely involving black groups. Others (Sinason, 2002; Badouk-Epstein, Schwartz, & Wingfield-Schwarz, 2009) have included abuse within white, middle-class satanist groups. It is interesting the way those concerned with the reality of this kind of abuse always use the term "satanic" abuse—bringing a Dennis Wheatley atmosphere into the discussion! We do not call abuse by a priest "God" abuse—we know it is the human. There has been a clever attempt to stir up religious fears by using the term "satanic". Satanism is a legal belief system and as I repeatedly point out, there are satanists who would never hurt anyone, and abusers within larger mainstream religions make up a far greater proportion.

Whilst courts have prosecuted cases of abuse within a belief context, clinical and social understanding of the lifelong impact of trauma is a separate trajectory to a court deciding, beyond reasonable doubt, whether A did something to B. With alleged sexual crime there are often only two witnesses who were present at the scene. Providing adequate evidence, and especially when the alleged victim has a mental health history, is difficult. However, it is only through the slow dissemination of clinical research (which is rarely based on court findings) that it becomes safer for victims to come forward, for judges and juries to understand more, and for adequate evidence to be obtained.

To be publicly wrongly accused of abuse is an abusive experience and there have been painful examples of this. However, these need to be differentiated from many examples provided by small vocal false memory groups (which include allegedly innocent family members); this is because many cases they publicise are ones they themselves have made public and in which their alleged family accusers (usually females) have not made public other than under pseudonyms (Sinason, 1998).

How then can clinicians show the nature of steps forward in treatment in ways that protect survivors (and their alleged abusers) whilst staying outside a court arena?

Freud took enormous care with protecting the real subjects of his case studies but even before the internet, detractors were seeking to uncover and publicise their real names and backgrounds. Literary and clinical grave robbers are rarely conducting this research to aid knowledge.

Sadly, it has been far more to discredit the testimony of the writer and those that tried to provide help. Whilst a large hospital can publish findings that include results from hundreds of patients, small intensive units are in a harder position.

This means that whilst it would have been clinically far more coherent to provide a single person case study from Lincolnshire and a pioneering one which inspired the work and could show all the exact interventions and personnel involved in the work, this would not be safe for any such client.

Professor Susie Orbach (1997) aided the whole professional field, which struggles with this problem, by providing not only the idea of amalgamated clinical material, which has existed for many years, but also a form of faction, in which like a novelist, she provided a fictional therapist and patients as the basic structure into which she could input her brilliant theoretical and clinical ideas.

Whilst the first person writing comes from people with a formal diagnosis of DID using pseudonyms, the other chapters make careful use of faction and amalgamation. As a result of these important publications giving voice to survivors, we hope this makes the environment safer for people to write about their own clinical experiences.

The clinical staff practise the methods described in the book but again, to ensure safety, names have been changed and a mixture of faction and amalgamation has been used. The composite picture provided highlights the way in which residential pioneering units can enrich and improve the lives of people with DID who are not safe in their current homes. Hopefully it also provides extra confidence to inpatient units and residential homes that would like to include people with DID in their patient group.

A remarkable editorial in the *Journal of Trauma and Dissociation*, "Ethical standards, truth and lies", (Brand & McEwan, 2016), scientifically supports the work of Cheit and others which shows how an unbalanced perspective has spread in which victims are seen as vulnerable to implanted memories, repressed or delayed memories cannot be trusted, and those who would help them are criticised and undermined.

Those who need a safe place to live are rarely finding sanctuary. The internal struggle is hard enough without clinicians and their patients having to deal with external shortage of adequate provision, fuelled in part by lack of training and understanding of DID. Hopefully this book will join others Karnac has bravely published in making it easier for survivors to speak and gain treatment.

CHAPTER ONE

Starting out

We need your help, we need your aid
Because we are so much afraid
The bad ones talk and hurt us so
We have no safe place to be and go
We're wanted dead we're wanted gone
The road is wearisome and long
We need to find a strengthened place
An open and a friendly space.

We need you to hear what we say
And help us find a better way
The dark ones always in a crowd
Follow us and they are proud
To hurt and maim and poison too
Like we're the dog dirt off their shoe
They never care about us so
Do you know somewhere safe to go?

The information in this chapter is relevant to a number of people with DID and will be presented in such a composite way as to enable the maintenance of confidentiality for the individuals concerned. Safety is always an issue for people with DID, who have survived abuse and trauma, often in a family context, and usually with some continued threat. The stories and the information informing the plans are those found most often with the client group.

The assessments by tertiary centres specialising in DID are usually the starting point for planning a support package. They highlight the level of trauma and complexity of the client and there is an immediate realisation of how carefully a plan would have to be made if it were to be effective. The level of self-harm and "calling out" to attend rituals for some people is a significant concern such that only a twenty-four-hour package of support has any chance of success. The attachment to dangerous groups can lead to people being called out to attend ritualistic events of an abusive kind. Hospital stays, although twenty-four hours, have often not proved to be useful or helpful. Supervision and support in hospital is not twenty-four hours and people can still be taken to rituals. There is also an impersonality in hospital that can fail to meet any attachment needs. Trust is difficult and can be absent.

Consequently, the basic requirements are just not there. Many people have tried, over many years, to diagnose and provide a suitable treatment but none has been fully successful. The people who have benefitted most from interventions are those who have had access to individual intensive psychotherapy and are living in a relatively safe environment.

An example of a plan follows (see Chapter Six for more details). Initially, Carly (an amalgam name to protect confidentiality) was seen for outpatient therapy in a local health centre. These were two-hour sessions once a week. After a period of time in hospital and respite care, it was decided that she could have a care worker at home all the time. This helped but it was difficult to maintain workers who were aware of the difficulties and able to provide the right level of support. They needed to be the same workers and this proved too hard. They also needed to be trusted and this proved too much for Carly and her other parts. Eventually the CEO of the Trust that was supporting her agreed to a specialist provision that would meet all her needs. This was a 24/7 supported living package with therapy twice a week. This was innovative and very brave of the CEO, who was known for her ability to think creatively to solve a difficulty and to make it person-centred.

Supported living packages are more usual with the learning disability population than they are for people in the mental health services, so it was helpful to reframe DID as a potentially chronic disability. Carly also has a physical disability, which helped in the establishment and recognition of her needs. Big questions were about the level of support needed and who could provide it, along with suitable therapy, psychiatric support, GP support, and care management.

It is important to recognise the difference between supported living and a residential placement. Although the plan is for twenty-four-hour support, it does not have the restrictions and shared space elements of residential care. It also allows the individual to keep their benefits and pay their own bills, hence keeping a level of responsibility and a sense of an ordinary life. The authorities then only pay for the staff support element and the therapy. Everything else is covered by rent allowance, disability benefits, and income support. The legal regulations are different too, as well as staffing levels. In residential care there are requirements that can be restrictive. Staff support is often at the level of two staff to a room of twenty people. This can't provide the consistent message that is required for the treatment of someone with DID.

Once it was decided that the best option for Carly was to provide a supported living environment that kept her safe, the plans could be put into operation. There are four elements to the trauma-informed care (TIC) model and all needed equal attention if the plan was to have a chance of succeeding.

Trauma-informed care

The first element is a safe place to live. We decided in our "amalgam" to provide an example of someone with a physical disability to do justice to the environmental adjustments needed, and, of course, many people with intellectual disabilities also have extra physical needs. Carly is a wheelchair user so suitable housing was needed, in the right place, with the right space, and where it was possible to recruit enough staff. A bungalow was identified that looked appropriate. It belonged to the family of an elderly person who had passed away and was available for a long-term tenancy. The bungalow has since changed ownership but the tenancy has continued and is safe for as long as it is needed.

Whatever the disability or needs, it is important that suitable property is found, in a safe place, and feeling right for the person involved. There will always be traumatic triggers to be considered, even to things like gardens and trees, so these must be taken into account. There needs to be a short-term tenancy at first, to ensure that the place will feel right, but with the option for it to be long term when the individual is settled. If it doesn't feel right it won't fulfil the need to be a secure base (Bowlby, 1979). You can see that it is very different from the usual housing provision.

Moving day for Carly was hard work and helped by everyone working together to achieve the goal. It was possible to arrange for one of the new support workers to be there to help pack and to travel with Carly to the new home, then to help unpack and settle in. The chaotic lifestyle that Carly was used to meant that there were lots of things that were in varying states of mix-up so it took a little while to achieve some order. The previous owner of the new house had left some pieces of furniture which were good quality and useful, so they were brought into use and helped with storage space for books and suchlike. The house was fully carpeted and curtained so that was not a problem. It had a conservatory that was quickly brought into use as a safe place for the younger alters and this was fitted out with toys, craft materials, and drawers for each alter's belongings. The availability of space for the young alters to be in and feel seen and valued is an essential part for many people with DID. Some do not have child alters, or can't access them, but most have, and, as they are the ones who were traumatised initially, it is necessary for them to have space within which to process that trauma. It has been my experience that this space is used well, when it is needed, and generally looked after by the adult alters, as they respect what their young alters need.

The second component of a therapeutic package is enough staff to establish a safe team. It was important for Carly and others that these were people who were already employed by the support provider, so as to ensure that no potential abusers applied for the jobs. Individuals were identified from the existing workforces and transferred to work in this specific service. They need to be selected for their ability to be calm and accepting, not domineering but able to make decisions and be reassuring that they are competent to keep everyone safe. The shift pattern was afternoon, sleepover, and morning shift for most of the time. Sometimes there would be a change in the morning or a new person would come for the sleepover and morning. It was arranged to allow for the maximum involvement with the community, allowing time to use public transport for shopping trips and other outings. There were considerations about transport generally as public transport was not ideal, so some staff needed to be drivers and able to put the wheel-chair, where relevant, in and out of the car. It has been found helpful to use a conflict management scale at interview in order to identify staff who are neither too timid, nor too authoritarian. If they are too timid they will potentially be bullied by hostile alters who may identify with the perpetrators; and, if too dominant, they may activate memories of abuse and past trauma.

The third component is staff training and support. All staff are pro-vided with an opportunity to attend a support group on a weekly basis. They need to be able to do this in work time or be paid if they come in on non-work days. In addition they need access to the level two training in trauma-informed care (www.frankishtraining.co.uk) and are encour-aged to complete this. This course helps them to understand the pro-cesses involved in the development of a sense of self, enabling them to explore the issues of multiple selves. Later on there can be some specific training sessions around the specific needs of the individual. For this later training it is very helpful if the client themself can contribute as this brings the issues alive for the staff, enabling them to reach a deeper understanding. There will always be the potential for some tension but, if the staff are recruited for their suitability, trained, and supported, the potential for a successful living plan and treatment is there. Over time it may be possible to reduce the staffing component and this can be an aim. If it isn't possible, it is still better to have a settled life with staff support, than a chaotic and dangerous life, maybe short, without adequate support.

The fourth, and final, piece of the puzzle is individual therapy. This is usually provided twice a week for a long time (years). During the sessions it is possible for all of the alters to have an opportunity to speak and be listened to. Over the years in excess of thirty alters can make themselves known, and some stay as host for weeks or months or years. In addition to the face-to-face contact there can be text and email contact. These afford another channel for use between sessions. Of special importance can be a goodnight text from the therapist to a younger alter, which is reassuring and confirming. The therapy aim is to help the person with DID to become able to live comfortably with who they are. There may be a wish to integrate, there may not. Facing the traumatic memories and living with them is a primary aim. Valuing all the selves is another, with acceptance of the need to have them there to fulfil their function in the maintenance of the whole. This happens in the context of a safe attachment figure in the therapist.

The TIC model is based on an acceptance that trauma experienced early in life, and compounded later in life, interferes with the development of a stable sense of self. At its most extreme the personality development splinters into many selves and DID is the result. The presentation varies according to the earliest trauma, with those traumatised before the age of three or four being the most distressed and disturbed.

Early emotional development

The model used is based on the work of Margaret Mahler and her book, with colleagues, *The Psychological Birth of the Human Infant* (2000). This work has been extended by Frankish (2013) to arrive at a model for understanding, and measuring, delayed or arrested emotional development in adults. Most of this work has been with people with learning disabilities, but it has relevance for anyone suffering trauma in the early stages of life, between biological birth and psychological birth. Frankish has developed a tool for measuring the stage of emotional development. In individuals with DID, there will be some alters who have reached a higher level of development than others, but the condition itself, of multiple selves, indicates a failure of the individuation process, so it is a useful theory to consider.

The first stage to look at is called symbiosis and indicates a very close relationship between the parent and child. This is the first building block and my experience of people with DID would suggest that this one is probably traversed adequately. People who don't even have this would potentially be seriously sociopathic which we don't see in DID. If they didn't care they wouldn't hurt.

The second stage is called differentiation and relates to the age from a few weeks to about ten months in traditional development. It is characterised by self-referenced behaviours, lack of seeking interaction with others, but responsive to contact from others. We all have some differentiation behaviours like hair twiddling, nail biting, and suchlike. People with DID will potentially have some alters at this stage, who have been traumatised in the first year of life, either by neglect or fear.

The third stage is practising and relates to the age range of approximately ten months to fifteen months. The relevant behaviours are repetitive and can look obsessional. They are based on competence. The person does what they know they can do and repeats this behaviour until another behaviour is learned or becomes available. There are lots of repetitive behaviours seen carried out by different alters. It is clear that some alters can do some things and other alters can't do them, but can do other things. One alter may be an obsessional cleaner, another may be a repeat self-harmer and so on. People traumatised at this age will have alters who are associated with the skills that were available to them at that time, and the behaviour of each alter will be stuck with the patterns that felt safe, or was a response to feeling unsafe. This stage is still relatively self-referenced and not very interactive, so the individual alters who are at the practising stage will not have skills to negotiate or choose, but will be stuck in patterns that are an end in themselves.

The fourth stage is early rapprochement and marks the beginning of an interactive style. Another person is needed for the give and take behaviours that are prominent at this stage, which is mostly pleasant and fun. The alters from this stage will be happy to play games, do things together, be guided in activities, and express their own wishes. They are also likely to react badly to being left, as they have just begun to value the presence of another. People who have been abandoned, neglected, or tortured at this chronological age will be very traumatised and this will show in alters who need to always know who is looking after them, whether they can be trusted not to abandon them, and won't hurt them or pass them on to abusers.

The late rapprochement stage follows and is a continuation of the move to independence. There is an increase in decision making with the necessary reasoning and weighing up of alternatives. There is development of the ability to think about consequences and the "if-then" phenomenon. At this stage individual alters may be happy to be, and enjoy being, alone for periods of time, able to hold on to feeling safe for progressively longer periods. Support staff may find themselves rejected and will need to learn to accommodate the changing demands, not expecting too much, but not being overprotective. If an alter at this stage is threatened in some way, or begins to feel insecure, they are likely to switch to a younger alter who will feel able to ask for help or support. It becomes an adaptive way of functioning, even though there is not total integration. Between them the alters manage to have their needs met so long as support staff recognise them. The problems come if the person with DID is apparently coping, then switches, and the other people around don't recognise it for what it is. This can lead to a major breakdown of trust and is probably the most common situation around admissions to hospital as the presentation will be of someone becoming irrational, whereas what has really happened, is that they have used the dissociative defence that they learned to use as a small child in order to survive.

The final stage, individuation, is only possible if the person with DID reaches a state of integration. This can happen and be held for periods of time, but may be lost at times of increased stress. It requires the ability to trust the self to be competent and able to trust, so a big ask for someone who has experienced serious traumatic abuse in early childhood. Many people without DID may struggle to stay fully adult all the time, secure in their identity and place in the world. Someone with many alters will have even more difficulty, but can reach an understanding of when they are able to do it, and what the triggers will be that challenge the more mature state. They can then use their cognitive ability to make plans and ensure that they stay within their comfort zone.

Summary and implications

So, to summarise, someone with many alters will have some alters at all of these developmental stages. These will relate to the trauma they experienced at the relevant chronological age of the developmental stage, bearing in mind that the earlier the trauma, the more interference there will be with the overall process, so there could be an overall delay in development. Support staff and therapists will need to learn which alters are at which stage and respond appropriately to that person, as well as help them to work out what it was in the environment that activated that alter. For example, a more adult alter may suddenly feel that no one is there and switch to a young alter who can more easily ask for help. Alert staff will recognise what caused that to happen, and while welcoming the child alter, will gradually help the building up of a picture that is comprehensive and has the opportunity to lead to integration. Some will be afraid that the younger ones are killed off in some way, so gentle support to recognise that we all have integrated child selves that we need to look after, and have the ability to warn us of danger, so they are not lost.

The implications for support staff of the emotional developmental model of understanding are significant. The recognition of the emotional needs of the alters helps with day-to-day behaviour and support, as well as enabling the integration process. As each frightened part is enabled to live in the world and experience positive support and no punishment, there is potential for them to grow individually through the stages, although some will stay stuck, carrying the trauma that they carry, which is too much for others to even look at.

It is clear that the process is very complex and there will be lots of false starts, times when it looks like progress is being made, for it all to come crashing down with a very young or withdrawn alter taking over as host for quite long periods. This can be very hard for support staff and others to work with but, if it can be understood as a reaction to a triggering event, it can be faced up to and the pain shared, which then enables the person with DID to begin to trust. It may be that an alter who is there to do some specific work will then be integrated and not reappear unless those circumstances occur again. Again it can be helpful for the host at the time to have a cognitive appreciation of what has happened, and then to gradually process the emotional responses, which involves facing the past trauma, which is so very hard for them.

Bringing the model alive

The summary above gives a description that can apply to anyone living with the issues. An attempt will now be made to bring the ideas alive with real examples. Whilst few people will have memories before age four, Bethie is an alter who was traumatised aged two and now cries, sucks her thumb, and tries to talk. She even tries to text sometimes with very baby-like spelling. Her memories are of being dropped on her head and she describes having tubes attached to her to give her what sound like electric shocks. Most of the time she is very withdrawn and alone, but now and again will seek contact, so is at the early rapprochement stage of development. She carries, for the whole system, the early pain and distress of the very little girl. Another alter, Scarred, is profoundly disabled, probably in response to torture and cruelty, but may be an alter from the prelingual stage of development, at the differentiation level. She communicates by blinking in response to questions, so has some higher cognitive level functioning.

There are lots of early rapprochement alters, and this is likely to underline traumatic events before age three and then, having become stuck at this developmental level, more and more alters arriving to help to cope with the pain and fear. These alters need a lot of attention, affection and support. They struggle to trust, and are hypervigilant to danger, which is perceived as anything unexpected or related to past trauma. This is common to post-traumatic stress and to be expected. Each one has their own needs, their own triggers, and their own story. All the stories need to be told within the context of a safe and trusted relationship. The individual therapy becomes the place and it is not uncommon for a two-hour session to include eight or more alters, all with their own things to say, some triggered by each other.

Sometimes an alter will surface to correct the last one and they can end up disagreeing, but more often they come to add to the information. It becomes clear that some situations have been so traumatic that several dissociations have happened very quickly and they each have a part of the memory.

Sadly the stories are gory and terrifying, accounts of ritual abuse including sex, physical injury, babies being born and murdered, being made to drink blood and more. It quickly becomes apparent that dissociation was the only way to survive and, had they not become multiple, they would have become psychotic. Presumably some do become psychotic and end up as chronic patients. Some commit suicide to get away from the pain. Dissociation is a survival mechanism that works but leaves the person and their internal system vulnerable and often misunderstood.

Some systems have alters of both genders and also animals. Together they form a whole personality, with the personality parts clearly delineated. An aim of therapy can be to facilitate integration of all the parts to become a whole integrated personality. However, others will find it extremely difficult to part with their alters, and will instead accept the parts and help them to communicate with each other so as to manage in the world. This seems to be the more usual outcome. There will be functioning adult parts who can manage day-to-day responsibilities, and may even be able to work and earn a living. Animal parts can be very protective and don't want to leave, or be abandoned by the more adult parts. Some alternative gender parts can struggle with gender-specific elements, like being male in a female body and coping with menstruation. All of the parts have a role, some protective, some quite angry and demanding in a way they would never have dared in the first instance with the abuser, or they were, and were severely punished for it. They may have nightmares. Any of them can have flashbacks and these can feel very real, as if the event is happening again. It can be frightening to witness these, but essential that the therapist stays with it and learns more about what happened. With individuals who have no awareness of their alters, the therapist then has to share with others what they have learned from the flashbacks, and help them to process the horror. Timing for this is critical and great care is taken not to traumatise others with information they are not ready for.

In my experience people with DID will often draw very graphic descriptions of traumatic events and these can be shown to other parts if they are ready to see them. It is important to remember that this is not on the level of forensic evidence but tools to be used in therapy to aid understanding of what happened so as to help with the processing of the memories. It is not possible to take away what has happened, so a way of living with what cannot be changed has to be found.

Sadly most people with DID allege abuse within the family context. Their parents were members of a satanist cult and their children were taken along to be used. Some of them were used as "breeders" within the cult, expected to produce babies for sacrifice or to increase the membership of the cult. They will have helped with the torture and exploitation, failing to protect or provide love and support for their children. Most people who manage to survive and escape will be terrified of being taken back. But most will have alters who would willingly go, as they have been programmed to obey and go when they are called. This latter situation is the main reason for providing 24/7 support. This can be reduced to telecare for some people, so long as the response to the electronic call can be answered in time.

Police involvement

Over the recent past there has been a more positive approach from the police. At first they did not believe the stories of ritual abuse, and abuse by high-ranking people. As more evidence has been discovered, the attitude has improved. However, there is a real shortage of hard evidence and the implication is that most of the perpetrators from the satanist cults are clever and well connected, making it very difficult to gather evidence against them. It is also very difficult when one alter may deny what another alter has said. Both can be telling the truth, they may not have been present at the same time. This is very hard for ordinary police officers to work with. Clive Driscoll, retired police officer from the Metropolitan Police, has taken the issue very seriously and his book helps us to understand better what the police are dealing with. Some people with DID have not been believed when presenting at the police station after sexual assaults, and may not have forensic evidence collected. This leaves them feeling not believed and desperate, sometimes leading to a suicide attempt, or an actual suicide.

The police do, at times, try to trace the perpetrators from the evidence that the person with DID has, but, sadly, most of them have memories from childhood that they can't adequately describe, and others have been deliberately deceived in relation to places and names. There is a common thread of perpetrators being hooded and robed, making them impossible to identify. Details often stick in the memory, of a colour or a smell, or being very cold, or of wood panelling and suchlike. But these are not usually enough for the police to work with. I have usually found them willing to trace social services records for evidence of children's services being involved and health records to see if there are any records of births and other healthcare. One DID person I worked with had no early health records that anyone could find. Another showed that social services made calls to the house but didn't take action. It does seem as though the parents are very determined to leave no trace of what has happened. Or they could be afraid for their own safety if their role in the cult has been to provide children as slaves.

Conclusion

Setting up a new service for someone who has had a chaotic and terrifying life is possible. It is also possible to maintain it with the right level of support for staff and all the four ingredients are vital to ensure that this is the case. The therapy is the main restorative tool but can only be effective if the other things are provided as well. The individuals who have informed this work have been able to live a good life in relative peace once their basic security was addressed. Sadly they can never be fully free and may be triggered at any time to go to the cult, self-harm, or even commit suicide. The presence of the support is vital and may be needed, to some extent, for life. If so, it is in recognition of the extreme vulnerability that follows from not knowing who you are, or who you might be, from one minute to the next.

CHAPTER TWO

A usual bumpy road to treatment

What did I do wrong to deserve such abuse
Sometimes I wonder what is the use
In trying to understand people and world
Evil is the only plan that is unfurled
People are cruel and hurt and dismay
People are just there to ruin your day
I don't understand this world oh so cruel
Everyone tried to maim and to rule.

Life should not competitive be
It should be good and of abuse free
So I don't understand where this abounds
Just like I do not understand sound
People can hurt with words and not heal
People can be unjust and not real
And when you cant talk it just is not fair
To have dictatorial people there.

Lots of loud sound gets right in my face
Just like the making of life like a race
Be kind instead of horrid and wrong
Tune your mind into a different song
Do not be clipped but open your door
Be receptive and then you will soar
No abuse, no shouting, you frighten my world
And then a planet of peace can be unfurled.

This chapter is about the impact on services of the client with DID. It is based on the experience in a small northern town, with services and staff trying to make sense of a person they can't make sense of. The possibility of organised criminal ritual abuse does not come easily to mind and, even when it is considered, there is a reluctance to believe that it could be present.

In childhood there are referrals to social services, usually from school or neighbours, but the abusers are very good at convincing the authorities that everything is all right and children are missed, not given the protection they need. There is more recognition of ritual abuse in 2016 than there was in the twentieth century but it is still disbelieved by many. This leaves the children isolated and afraid. The cost to the services can be high, with many visits and meetings to decide what to do and then finding there is nothing they can do. Most people with DID will have fat files in children's services but will not have been given the protection they needed.

At age sixteen they can make a choice and the brave ones do, taking themselves to the authorities and asking for help. Supported living can then be provided to enable them to make a start on their adult life. It is unlikely that a sixteen year old will be able to tell anyone what has happened to them and, even if they can, they may not be believed. But at least they are making a start. This is when the programmed alters become active and start to take the body back to the abusers for rituals, particularly around the summer solstice and Halloween, but there will be other crucial dates as well. The non-programmed alters, including the host alter, can't tell anyone for fear of reprisals from the cult, but will present at hospital A&E departments frequently with injuries, self-harm, and suicide attempts. These are a cry for help that is generally not heard. They may gain a reputation as a problem or a time-waster and receive less than optimal care in the system. Although the statistics are not available, it seems very likely that a significant number of them succeed in taking their own lives.

As adulthood looms there is less support. People with DID often have physical disabilities as a result of the abuse they have endured and may, then, receive support as a disabled person. This helps but does not recognise the DID and the support needed for that. Disability benefits do allow people to live, to have housing, and to have enough to eat. However, this money is also sought by the cult and they frequently find themselves paying out for things they don't need and getting into debt. Sometimes they receive direct payments for support hours but then spend the money on other things, leaving the local authority to pay the bills twice. This creates more animosity and interferes with the care situation. The individual is seen as manipulative and demanding with professionals struggling to work out what to do and, more importantly, to work out what is happening and why nothing seems to work.

A typical situation will be around an admission to an acute mental health NHS unit. The individual is admitted from A&E with serious self-inflicted wounds. They say that they have been taken for a ritual involving sexual activity and sacrifice. The ward staff find this hard to believe and decide that there are symptoms of psychosis. So begins the mismanagement that can continue for many years. I am not speaking here about the small number of cases of fictitious disorder. They are another group. Often the admission will be to a unit away from the home area because of bed shortages and then necessitating interactions with a whole new set of people. The police may be asked to come in and interview the patient to follow up the claim of sexual assault. These may not be police from the local force but from the locality of the mental health unit, causing yet more confusion. The alter who is present, at the time of the interview, doesn't know where it happened as the cult made sure that the location could not be identified. The police officer says there is not enough evidence and persuades the alter present to retract the complaint. Another door closes and justice is not available.

After the police have effectively said it didn't happen there can be a reduction in positive feelings towards the patient. They don't seem to be psychotic. The police don't believe they were abused. No one knows how to understand the condition or how to make an intervention plan. Then someone suggests that the condition is borderline personality disorder (BPD). There are observable changes in mood (as different alters come and go) and these are seen as the mood swings of BPD. There is self-harm and presentation at A&E and these are seen as attention-seeking behaviour often seen, and misunderstood, in BPD. A decision is then made to refer for dialectical behaviour therapy (DBT) in a group. Attendance at a group on a regular basis is a huge ask for someone with DID, where they have no way of knowing which alter makes the agreement to attend, and which one may be around on the day, with or without the knowledge of the session, or how to get there. Failure to attend is interpreted as lack of commitment and the next attendance at A&E is treated with hostility because of what is seen as a lack of engagement in their own recovery.

Sometimes individuals with DID are seen as being possessed by demons and this can arouse the interest of different churches. Attempts to exorcise the demons can be very traumatic, as they clearly are not demons, but other personalities. Any attempt to make them go away will be experienced as death-making and be very distressing. On a more positive note, some churches offer fellowship and acceptance and can be safe places to be. Belonging is important, but the similarities of religious rituals to abusive rituals can also be disturbing. Contact at the right time with the right people can be very beneficial and therapeutic. At the wrong time and with the wrong people it can be exploitative and dangerous to the mental wellbeing of the person with DID.

And so it goes on, getting worse and worse, with relationships breaking down and despair increasing. The individual with DID is desperately seeking understanding and help. They don't understand their own condition and suffer extreme confusion and fear as they find themselves with memory loss and not knowing how they got to where they are. The loss of time that alters report is evidence of DID. It seems that the mind is so compartmentalised that there is no leakage from one alter's knowledge to another. One thing that helps with this is a communication book, where alters can write to each other, and there can be the development of shared knowledge. But it needs someone to understand and recommend this. In the absence of such knowledge, there is only fear and confusion with a deterioration in relationships as the patient doesn't feel helped and the staff feel that the patient is being difficult and deliberately not being compliant. It is common for ward rounds and multidisciplinary team meetings (MDTs) to dissolve into chaos or splitting as the various professionals grapple with something that is uncommon and challenging, trying to find a way forward.

What usually happens is that the individual with DID becomes a revolving door patient. They move from acute admission, to home, to respite, to home, to friends, to acute care, to physical acute care, then mental health acute care, and so on and so on. It would not be uncommon to find that by the age of 30 an individual has had more than twenty admissions to hospital, numerous stays in respite, a period of time in a care home, multiple home addresses, and be no further forward in terms of a diagnosis or a plan. It becomes very difficult to make and keep friends. Life becomes very lonely.

The cost becomes prohibitive. Inpatient days are approximately £500 a day, with day services at £120 a day, outpatient appointments

£130 each, and A&E £130 a visit (all costs approximate and subject to local variation). Respite care will be approximately £600 a week and home support based on two hours a day about £200 a week. This chaotic arrangement comes to approximately £70,000 a year and does not produce any gain. It can continue for years like this, with risk of death increasing, disruption of services for other people increasing, and no improvement in the mental health of the person with DID. These figures don't include the cost of MDTs (which are expensive) or the cost of management time used to try and come up with a solution, or staff training days that may be included to try to help. Nor is there any allowance here for therapy that sometimes is provided, on an outpatient basis, by psychologists or psychotherapists. Then there is the cost of the care manager and crisis teams who invariably get involved from time to time.

Another factor is physical health. Most people with serious abuse histories have a range of physical conditions as well, and these take up lots of GP and practice nurse time, which is another expense. Multiple pregnancies and miscarriages feature significantly and usually without the benefit of any medical care. This and eating disorders are common and lead to more visits to services, more confusion about underlying causes. If the individual is still being taken for rituals, there will potentially be more pregnancies and early inductions for sacrifices.

Clearly GP support stays the same with the holistic approach, but becomes more orderly and average as the individual settles down more to feeling supported and not pressured to seek help. Hopefully there will also be a willingness to seek medical help with long-term conditions that haven't been properly addressed. Attending appointments and following medical advice is one of the indicators that they are putting a value on themselves.

Although a holistic approach can look expensive at £100k a year, this is the total cost of support and therapy, and leads to improvement in mental health and the possibility of being able to lead an ordinary life. In time the cost reduces as the person with DID becomes able to manage their own life and possibly to work and earn their own living. Ending the chaos seems like a good goal in itself.

It may have been noticed that there is no mention of family in any of the above. Many people with DID, according to their reports, have been abused within their family and breaking away is an essential part of their survival. Consequently they have no one to call on when distressed or in danger, as making the call will increase the danger. They have no support, except from professionals, and struggle to feel valued and to develop feelings of self-worth. The holistic approach establishes a small team of support workers who become key attachment figures, additional to the therapist, and provide a growth experience in a nurturing environment. It takes time for trust to grow and when it does real progress can be made. This small team of staff need to be supported to manage their reactions to what they learn about DID and the criminal ritual abuse that causes it, and to keep going when they are rejected and vilified by alters who don't recognise them. They become the substitute family and provide real-life experiences that lead to growth.

CHAPTER THREE

Life—what's that?

How do we even prepare to begin
To tell of a life that is without sin
The child not at fault and yet so abused
Treated liked dog dirt and totally used
Hurt and controlled and tortured and pained
Rituals glory the bad people gained
So the child broke in pieces with lots of new names
Because of torturer's spiteful evil games.

The battle to live began at our birth
The child constantly fighting to even have worth
The horrors that happened splitting her mind
Into children and adults, animals of all kinds
The fight for their freedom constantly aflame
Until one day they were rescued and their freedom came
Many years came and many years went
Until one day a new life was sent ...

To most people in the world, I exist as one person—that is what society sees and thinks I actually am. But to those who know me, we are much more than one person—we are many inside one body. This is because we have Dissociative Identity Disorder (DID), and have many alternate personalities (alters). As a collection of alters we switch in and out of the body, and are many different ages, both male and female, and animals who keep our body safe, all with different abilities and roles. Within the following writing by ourselves, you will notice changes between the words I and we. This signifies switching between alters, which we felt was important to happen for chronological continuity and for everyone inside our body to have their say who wants to. Also, direct quotes by any alter are indented in a different font. Everyone within our system has been silenced for too long, and now it is time for our truths to be known.

We were born but had no life. We understand from the one person we trusted, we had no one to tell us we were loved; no one to pick us up and let us know we were good enough; and had nothing but World War Three for a home. It is hard for anyone to grow up unwanted but to be also abused in every way possible including ritually, makes life a living hell. The hardest thing out of it all now looking back is to know that no one wanted that tiny child and that she was not good enough for anyone. That tiny child that should have been whole and cared for, became split into tiny pieces that we now know to be alters or other personalities, which goes under the diagnosis of DID. The babies in our DID system still cry for the love that they needed then, now. It makes us so angry, because they deserved so much more than they got in life.

An excerpt from a poem, written by a young alter:

> They hurt you and they grab you and they tug into your hair
> Until all of you is gone and you know that you're not there
> Until you float away and are gone for years and years
> Away from all pain and grief, the sorrow and the tears
> No one knows the pain you feel and no one would believe
> That there is no ending and way to feel relieved

When we were three, the mother of us wanted us dropped on our head and killed, and held one of our little alters by the ankles upside down, threatening to do so. We do not know why she did this, but we have asked that question many times, to ourselves, and we have this on good authority from a witness to the memory, that it happened, and B who is three remembers it vividly. Consequentially over time, the authorities were involved but no one moved us away from the so-called family unit. There was then a messy divorce aged six including sexual abuse from our mother's new partner, and further physical abuse from the mother, and we were left going back and forth between both sets of abusive "family". We even ran away between the two, but nowhere was safe. No one really wanted us except for what we could do for them, and with mind control programming and training thrown into it all, we were left a mess and this set us up for life—whatever that was.

> Ki woz scard ov th divors an tranin
> Ki neva no bowt hoo to trst
> It scari an ki swmd wa wiv the dolfis in ki hed
> Ki woz scard ov th mumi an ddi
> No wer woz saf

Translated, Ki (name changed to disguise her), a six-year-old female alter, wrote that she was scared of the divorce and mind control "training". She never knew who to trust and because she was scared and was unable to cope with such trauma, she imagined swimming away with the dolphins in her head, as a means of escape. She was scared of her mother and father, and for little Ki, nowhere was safe.

The mind control mentioned involved many forms of psychological procedures and hurt, with a lot of hypnosis thrown in. Everything from behavioural psychological elements of negative reinforcement and punishment, split brain techniques, spin programming involving spinning us upside down combined with hypnosis, to hypnotic states themselves were used on us, and with lasting effects. This form of training began when we were tiny, and we have a castle setup within our system with different alters in different hierarchies on different levels within the castle, now because of it. Wizard of Oz programming was also used on us, and we were an experimental case for them to do whatever they wanted with us. The coven had very clever trained people in these fields, who even created some alters that were trained to call back the coven and be accessed when required to go to them. It has damaged us for life, and our head feels like it will never be right because of it. We feel numb writing about this with shock and grief at what happened, that even nearly drove us to killing ourselves.

For years we had to endure rituals, such as being married to Satan at six years old, and many sexual, satanic, and hypnotic rituals left our body and mind a mess. Being married to Satan involved a six-year-old alter being married in a ritual ceremony to the evil one, and it being consummated with coven members afterwards, whilst hypnotic rituals involved being hypnotised and made to do horrible things during these times. We were totally alone and not wanted except what we could be used for. The grandmother was even scared of her own son's antics, and as a father, he was terrifying. Later she told them she was scared of him but would not move to safety. Some people wondered about what he got up to, but were too afraid to actually ask. Not one time did he ever say he loved us, and that is sorely felt.

Starting at a very young age, the bad people photographed us on a pornography level. These photos were taken of us, taken with a Polaroid camera, and distributed to the coven, much to our shame and embarrassment. The hurt and pain of knowing that this happened to us, especially for our male alters in a female body, is huge, and the constant wondering if these pictures are still in circulation somewhere, is a constant source of worry. Pornography is demeaning, and the people who do it treat you like a piece of meat on a slab, whilst others get you to act the part, and through the tears, you try, or know you are going to get beaten to a pulp.

We also had to take to the streets to make the coven and the family money via prostitution. This is not something we are proud of, but we were forced into it. It was a life of dread, and many of the customers were from the coven anyway. Half the time we had to dissociate to survive. It made us feel so dirty and unwanted and helpless. All we wanted to do was die. We were treated like nothing and made to feel like nothing but a piece of meat to be used. All the time, we were nothing but an object to be used, and to give pleasure to others, but the pleasure was never ours. They even started preparing us for this aged three by stretching us with metal rods, ready for what they wanted us to do.

One female who had her fill sexually with us aged eleven, used kitchen equipment on our sexual organs, to give us pain. She taught us about how to behave when you are pregnant and how to hide it from people. She started by pretending that she was playing doctors with our eleven-year-old alter H, and then used a doll to explain pregnancy to her. This was to prepare us for what was to come, but because of our DID the information was never passed on in our psyche and so it became a shock to every alter that subsequently became pregnant.

We were then brought up a breeder—which is someone who is used as a carrier of children for the coven to sacrifice. We know that this sounds almost unbelievable, and yet it is not a lie. Covens do not care whom they use as long as they satisfy their purpose. The people who forced us into this expected us to be a breeder akin to someone who has no feelings and an automaton if you will. But it is not possible when you bond with a child inside you. The love you feel far outweighs everything else you could ever experience. So when your children are taken away so cruelly it hurts like crazy. The pain numbs you out, and you cannot cope with it, which caused further splits and therefore personalities to develop. There are a number of inside people or alters who remember these harrowing experiences. To anyone who disbelieves that people could do such a thing, they need to think about the depravity of some human beings, and what they are capable of.

At times we were pregnant we were kept away from swimming, an activity done to keep looking normal. This was mostly in the wintertime between the marriage of the beast festival on 7 September and the following Good Friday. None of our children were carried to term, as Good Friday is a ritual date, and our children were required for those. Had we been swimming, we would have shown, and the coven were cleverer than that. We even tried to run away once to save the life of our unborn child, but got caught and taken back and hurt after the sacrifice had been done.

As previously mentioned, mind control was a daily feature of our very young life too. As a child we were trained hypnotically and in many experimental ways that would be too triggering for readers to describe, the omega death programme being the worst. This programme led us to overdosing, cutting, and bulimia among other things.

As a twelve year old, I was going through hell on earth, and for me, I wanted to hurt the body using food, bulimia and anorexia. Being made to eat things such as gone-off raw meat put me off food and was bad enough, but constantly being told I was fat and being weighed every day is enough to drive anyone to an eating disorder. People later in the body's life told me the dangers, but I did not care about myself, and took lots of laxatives as a result. I am getting over this, but even as we write, another programme is active, that is causing much pain to all of us. There are even people inside that are trying to stop us writing, which, in our view means it is imperative for our truths to be spoken.

Attachments were affected deeply because of all of these happenings. The only person that actually really cared about us was a godmother who was there to make the family and coven look normal and everything okay. She did not even know how important her role was however. Life was hard, because at school everything had to look idyllic even though it was not. Everywhere else, people knew what was happening to us, but did nothing—leaving us feeling desolate, unwanted, and alone. We did, however, used to talk to our godmother about abuse we were receiving, and she tried to help us as best she could, but she was too scared to tell the authorities. She did get a friend of hers who worked at the school we went to, to keep an eye on us when she could, however. She also had done nursing training, and used to talk to us about pregnancy, and having babies even though she never said anything. We were sure she knew when we were pregnant although she never used to mention it. A bond formed with her though, and she loved us like a daughter when she could, and some inside that remember her love her to bits. She kept us sane. Very often now, we wish that she was alive to come forward as a witness now we are safe, to put all the doubters of ritual abuse we have ever had in our life to rest. We have to thank them though, as like the godmother of us, they have made us stronger, able to cope with the bad memories.

One thing we will always be hurt and angry about, is that there were people who knew what was going on and yet did nothing. Some were blinkered by the fact that the family were good at stopping people knowing what was going on, and other people were too scared, like our godmother, to open their mouths and get us to a place of safety. Even the grandmother of us was too scared to tell anyone that her son was being abusive. Everything had to look normal, and safe even though it was really like World War Three. They even gave us a normal-looking life in front of people and the father of us kept his temper from people, as much as possible, but underneath it was very different. The fact still remains, however, that a number of people could have done something but did not.

It is important to note, though, that our family and other abusers within the coven took great pains to make everything look normal outside of the ritual abuse situation. They in fact had to, because if they did not, they would have been caught. This was hell on earth for us, because the pretence was hell on earth for us. K in our system recalls having to eat Chelsea buns, in front of other people somewhere where the coven operated and having to pretend to enjoy them, just to make bad people who made her bulimic look good in front of others. This was so cruel to her, because at twelve, it made a mess of her eating habits for life.

> It is the little things that hurt the most for me. Not being fed proper food, and not being loved by the people that should love you. Being neglected for numerous girlfriends, and being made to have sex customers who use you like an object. It is not a life … it's an existence, and one that stinks at that. If I had been told I had been loved all the little and big things would have paled into insignificance. And let's face it, being made to eat Chelsea buns to look normal for them is hardly such is it? I just wanted to throw them up.

To a certain extent, friendships had to look normal although people inside our system were able to run away from the family home at times and just be normal children and teenagers from the family home. We are especially indebted to three friends that helped us with computer games and normal life at their homes. They made life more bearable, in the midst of what they knew to be abnormal circumstances. After all, whose grandfather ties them up to stone posts for a game where you have to try to escape, in front of their friends? These friends however were steadfast and helped to keep us sane. We just wish they had realised that under very baggy clothes we were pregnant and terrified, and maybe they did, but the father did have a reputation for violence, so maybe that was why.

In our mid-teens someone inside finally got the courage to go to social services who got us out. This was after the godmother and a key abuser died. S, the alter in question, wrote:

> I had to be really strong, and put my foot down, and say this is not going to happen to me anymore. I did not know I was a we then, but I had an innate sense of needing to get myself safe, particularly after my latest miscarriage. It was hard telling social services because I had to tell the bare bones of what was happening, just to get safe. It was the only way I could get out.

Whilst we were still accessed and hurt every so often, it was still safer than what we had been used to. (The term "accessed" means being called back to the coven by means of, for example, triggers over the telephone, and specific alters being used to respond to them.) Our fellow alter who managed to get away for us will always have our admiration and gratitude for what she did for us, especially with the abuse she had received. She and others had also been asked to commit suicide by their own father and had still been strong enough to do this brave act of getting safer.

> I was so angry with the authorities for telling me that no one would foster sixteen year olds because they did not want them. Instead I was placed in a hostel for young people five miles away from the family unit, and he worked near where we were put, and I never felt very safe at all knowing I could see him at any time. In fact I went round the corner one day and saw him on his motorbike, and ran back terrified that he would hurt me. Knowing what the authorities had told me about him being violent when they notified him they had taken us, I had no intention of wanting to go anywhere near him. The social worker even talked me out of a sexual examination saying that it was not very nice and I would not want one.

A number of houses later with people not knowing about or understanding our DID, and we were severely self-harming and trying to kill ourselves, and not knowing why we wanted to (for which we later found out was part of our programming). Still feeling not wanted in places we were living in, there was never any acceptance, and we always felt the odd one out, moving around just to keep safe. We were also losing time and many clinicians had their various inaccurate opinions as to what was going on including one who quoted DID, but did not really understand us in her approach towards us. A in our system was most hurt by this and it is still unresolved for him if he is honest.

> This was a very dark time for us. All the inaccurate diagnoses were so annoying. I was offended when one clinician suggested borderline personality disorder because I knew it was more than that. I felt alone and lied to, and wondered if anyone understood me truly at all. Being a fifteen-year-old hothead male, I wanted to give them a piece of my mind. It was only when we got the DID diagnosis, that I finally felt okay with the world.

The core named body host was what we will call a "screen alter". She was an automaton if you will, programmed to tell people that she was lying to them when under force to throw them off the coven's scent. Her sarcasm also put people off knowing the truths of our abuse, but that was again just part of what she was programmed to be. Sometimes she would break through the programming to tell others what was happening, and told the complete truth, including to clinicians and the authorities, but they did not listen because of her role in our life. Also, at the time she was reporting things, people did not believe in ritual abuse, which made things even harder. This was way before things like Operation Yewtree, and people simply could not get their heads around this type of abuse. It was only when a DID expert became involved that the host would actually tell her truths and be believed. This was a landmark moment, and a turning point in our life, as to actually be believed after so long of being doubted, was such a relief, and we honestly felt like someone was actually taking our hand and walking with us.

Prior to the expert assisting us with our condition, we had a number of therapists who all tried their best to help us but no one recognised our DID, and many did more harm than good. We were a case for everyone to try various therapy methods such as person centred counselling, but not one of them was really trained in trauma-related conditions. One who did recognise our DID threatened to deprogramme us using hypnosis, especially the darker alters within our system, and this did no good at all, and only served to frighten the little ones inside. We were in a mess with no hope of anyone helping us.

We also had a number of inpatient admissions, on various mental health hospital wards, where many of the staff did not believe in DID. During these stays there were even alters who were trying to harm themselves on the wards, not caring what happened to them, but the staff did not even know on some occasions, that this was happening. Sure, they taught mindfulness, and gave us tasks to do on the ward, but they did not know what to do with our DID. This was a source of great distress for us, because we knew we needed help, but did not know what to do.

They treated us like a lump of dog dirt on their shoe. We were getting accessed when we left the hospital. I had to be alert when they let us leave the ward for a couple of hours. They gang-stalked us and watched for us coming out, and the ward staff did not even know. We tried to get an advocate within the hospital, but because we were not believed by the staff this service was not forthcoming much to my disgust. And because the screen alter did as she was told to do by staff and the authorities, it left us set up to fail, which was just not fair. We were totally alone in the world.

Various hospital staff were also not sympathetic to our disability. Being mental health staff, they did not know what to do. They tried to make us walk with a frame, even though we needed a wheelchair, and were not understanding of our needs. In our opinion, there needs to be more holistic care on hospital wards, as all patients on them very often have multiple needs that do not always appertain to mental health issues.

Umpteen times the then body host would end up in hospital with someone inside having overdosed but she did not know why. We think now that the accident and emergency doctors must have been fed up with seeing us at the time, and because they did not understand DID, they treated us quite often in a less than humane manner. We were just hurt and confused and did not really understand what was going on. All we wanted was someone to understand that we genuinely wanted to die, but they always treated us like timewasters because they did not actually seem to want to know about our condition. This is something we believe accident and emergency staff could do with training in, as there are many more than just us in the world with DID.

Shopping trips were also most confusing. Everything from children's toys to buttons and ribbon were being bought and then there were times we had no money and nothing to show for it at all. For someone who thinks they are an adult, a child's cuddly toy in their house for no reason is very confusing indeed. The reasons for this of course was that other alters were buying things, especially child alters to satisfy their needs and wants that they had not been allowed when the body was their age due to not having toys or them being burnt as punishments. Also, when the mother had fought for attention and given gifts such as toys they were encouraged not to be played with by the father and were burnt as well, so having toys that the little ones knew were value free and not going to get taken away was very important to them.

We were receiving threats upon our life as well, and although not believed by some people, who did not believe in ritual abuse and mind control, we used to hide in the house with the curtains shut because we were terrified. We had many threats including being gassed in our beds, to being killed with a sword, to having a gun to our head. During this time, we felt alone, and would have a friend stay, who did not know about the accessing, but kept us safe without knowing about it, and we are thankful for her help. There were times when the accessing was much less than others, but it depended who was around with us at the time. If they were strong people, or people they knew that would go to the police, they would stay away, but if we were on our own, then the rituals would start again, with alters being called out and going with them to be hurt. We had one terrifying night where windows were smashed and we were alone in the house, with a disability, trying to move away from where they were, but were followed around the house, window by window. Although we called the police, no one ever caught the culprit, even though a brick was thrown from one window nearly into the room beyond.

This was life, for what it was. People following us, making us unsafe and generally making us totally terrified. We moved again, but the same things happened and nothing was right. This was the point that DID specialists became involved with our case, and diagnosed us officially with DID. On the way to an appointment, we were even followed by someone involved in our abuse, and were terrified. The diagnostician however put us at our ease, talked to alters within our system, and read from writing that they had done. She performed her assessment and the diagnosis became official.

This brought with it much confusion at the diagnosis, and yet at the same time was a great relief. Whilst there were times of denial, and disbelief in the diagnosis, overall it was the best thing that could have happened to us. We finally had reasons, for all the lost time, and could finally know why we have different parts of us that we did not understand. We were given a reason to carry on. It felt like some of the darkness had lifted as someone understood our writings and drawings and made our life make sense.

With the diagnosis of DID, came a loss of friends. Everyone seemed scared of the condition, and when an angry alter came out and frightened them, each time we lost more and more friends. We told friends because it was such a relief to finally have a diagnosis, and we were eager for them to understand us better, but they were scared as they did not understand what we have. Being mainly from mental health groups, they focused on what was wrong with each other, and could not begin to get that DID was a trauma-related survival mechanism, to the abuse that we received. We were not very good with people because of losing time either, so we ended up living a very lonely life indeed.

> Having animal and male alters was really weird at first. Having angry alters that were dark and wanted to hurt the body was even stranger. I only knew myself and finding writing written by animals confused me greatly. Having males in the system was also something I hated as I was not comfortable with them. I just wanted to hide and not understand or know anything that was going on. At that time, I was happy to stay in denial, and keep my head in the sand. It was easier not to accept was going on, as I had become used to losing long periods of time, and thought this was better than knowing any of the others. It was all too scary for words.

Things continued to become worse and things were happening to us regularly, and the friend that came to stay deserted us, and after having a failed lodger, and a stay in residential care, we came upon Dr Pat Frankish, who seemed to totally understand our case. We would see her for therapy sessions, and alters would come out, and the then body host would frequently lose time. They described the danger they were in, and how they would not go out because they did not feel safe. They hid from the world, isolated and alone, and terrified of who might come and break windows this time. During the stay in the home, flies had also appeared in the home and fridge, and people inside were terrified that people had put them in there.

> R woz fritid bt wont to prtekt evrawon in th bdee
> R woz md an wontd to ror reeli lts lowd
> R woz upstid cs it no saf no wer

When interpreted, this was an eight-year-old animal alter of ours, who wanted to make it clear how unsafe she actually felt. She was frightened and wanted to protect everyone in the body. She was mad and wanted to roar loudly. She was also upset because nowhere felt safe.

It was after a long period of this hiding from the world that things changed for good. Amara Care turned our life around with the help of the local NHS and the man who authorised our funding, and we moved to a totally different life. Healing from the memories, and the possibility of a meaningful life became plausible …

CHAPTER FOUR

Setting up a service

hapter One describes what is required to set up a service for someone with DID and complex needs. This chapter will explore in more depth what is required to manage a service of this kind. The service provider's main experience has been in providing specialist twenty-four-hour support for those with a learning disability. They have used the same principles but have needed to adjust the thinking and behaviour when supporting someone with multiple alters. This chapter is going to explore further the four components of providing a trauma-informed package and how the provider developed services in this way.

Initial thoughts of supporting someone with many alters within the community are "Can it be done? Will it be safe for the individual and also staff? What rules/laws will govern this type of project? How will it be funded? What do we need to do?" The service provider was able to overcome many such issues through knowing that they had the support of commissioners of the service.

Trauma-informed care:
element one, a safe base—location and tenancy

Chapter One describes how a bungalow was secured within a small local community that became a satellite service from one of the other twenty-four-hour services. This enabled the provision of an additional pool of staff that could be called on in an emergency but also a place where Carly could go and socialise with others. It is possible to have services in isolation but, as there is an inevitable element of unpredictability, it would always be more beneficial to know back-up is available if required.

The service does not need to be registered as residential care. There are discussions required in relation to the signing of a tenancy agreement. In recent years more questions are asked around capacity to do this. As someone with DID can switch between capacity, a multidisciplinary decision including the main alter was required in order to check that Carly had the capacity to sign the tenancy. The tenancy was an assured shorthold tenancy, which meant it gave six months to see how the service developed, before changing to a continued tenancy with one month's notice either way. A long-term lease can be used but most landlords like to know there are exit strategies. As it was not known how Carly would react, the assured shorthold tenancy was what was used. As safety is the key issue, and building trust is essential, the property concerned needs to be owned by a trusted partner to ensure eviction is not implemented. There also needs to be agreement within the tenancy that if there is a breach to the tenancy, the advocate and the team will work at resolving disputes and not move to eviction. There may be changes in rental and costs for landlords, so it is essential that all legalities regarding the tenancy are in order before taking on the lease.

Staffing

Once the location of the property was decided it required twenty-four-hour staffing. The issues regarding staff are greater than a usual twenty-four-hour service as it needed to ensure, as much as possible, that staff were not involved in the cult. The providers also knew that Carly was being accessed by others so, as they knew she was moving, there was a possibility of them receiving requests for employment. As this is a high risk, some of the current staff were transferred to manage this service and they did employ some new staff. All staff go through the same process of completing application forms, face-to-face interview, written test, a psychometric test, successful enhanced DBS, and satisfactory references. If at any time there were concerns about anybody they would add a second interview with psychology. All staff at the service are employed by the same company. As a company registered with the care quality commission (CQC), formally all staff are required to complete initial training. As they transferred staff already trained this enabled a more fluent move. All staff required knowledge on supporting a person with DID as this was new to everyone. The clinical psychologist working with Carly provided some initial training and supported the staff team throughout the first three years.

Care plans

The key to success has been providing a person-centred approach where Carly (whoever they may be at any time) is in the centre. The staff have needed to have an open mind and be able to work with whoever presents at any particular time. Writing care and support plans initially was implemented by the psychologist with staff experience of relevant procedures. These were all viewed weekly and changed accordingly. It was important that within the bungalow there is a place of safety for staff that is the staff sleep-in room. This is because staff need to record things that happen that may not be necessarily good for Carly initially to know about. Over the years there is more joint work with updating care plans and sharing of information. This has grown as the trust between parties has developed. There are communication books, risk assessments, food records, and medication records similar to what would be found within a residential home, but only as it is a complex service for someone with complex needs in a tenancy. Records are required in order to know if one alter may be trying to harm another: for example, a dark alter may make the body eat something they shouldn't and make them all ill.

Day of the move

Planning was required for the moving day as it was not possible to hire a removal firm as they would be unknown to us so they used the handyman and a couple of staff that were to support Carly in the new home. There were a lot of belongings as Carly had several alters requiring different things. These gradually have been sorted through as there was a lot of material no longer required. Once moved, the staff were left with Carly to build a new relationship and grow together.

Police

As a community setting there is no link to the police but Carly was introduced to the local community police person and information shared that enabled the police to put in place a tag on the address to say that if a call was made regarding the premises police action is required. This was put in place for safety reasons in case the abductors tried to access X. The police were also involved with investigating allegations of abuse as Carly progressed through her therapy.

Staff support

The service is complex and one element that enabled staff to keep going with the service, particularly in times of crises, was staff support sessions. When Carly was very challenging verbally, self-harming, wanting to abscond, or very demanding, the staff had weekly support sessions with psychology to discuss issues and used the time as a debriefing session. They became more competent as time went on and a small core team became established as trusted "others". Over time new people have been able to be added and the client herself has been able to provide some training for them.

First three months

Initially the level of "fear" for everybody was very high. Staff were wary because of the unknown and the need to keep Carly safe. Management had to ask "What if it goes wrong?" and Carly herself said "they're going to get me". A key factor to contain the fear was the psychology input. Carly had weekly therapy and staff were encouraged to attend weekly staff support sessions. Also staff were all included in updating and sharing information to inform care plans.

Four to eighteen months

As time progressed, managing the service became easier as staff contained a "safe base" and understanding of what was happening with Carly. This means there was a core group of four staff with one of them leading the service. As all four attended staff support sessions and worked closely with psychology they began to see "alter changes" and could tolerate the "differences" displayed by Carly such as play alter, hostile alters, self-harm alter. The challenge now became "how do we support Carly to maintain her safety?" As Carly lived in the community, when out she was constantly "triggered" by events. As time progressed Carly felt able to discuss these issues and through the support of staff "believing" and "holding" Carly, with psychology support, processes began to look at criminal events being registered with local police forces. At the same time more health concerns were addressed that helped Carly to begin to integrate and move forward.

Over this time Carly decided to change her name by deed poll to an alter she felt comfortable with, and rejected her birth name. Another major challenge, other than the emotional wellbeing, was financial support. It became clear that previously Carly had been on direct payments and owed the authority a large amount of money. Carly, although adult, has alters aged from three onwards, which allowed providers to understand why Carly had got into financial difficulty. This started to interfere with therapy so a decision was made that Carly's care provider would act as appointee and support them all to manage the bills and finances. This was a little difficult to start with, but soon became easier. A long time ago Carly had her weekly allowance to go shopping and so on, and was able to tolerate this. When the financial pressure was removed, they began to engage better in therapy. The worry of court action had been removed.

Eighteen months to three years

When arranging care services there is always the risk of not being able to maintain enough staff of the right calibre. The service was quite lucky in that staff managed to stay connected throughout the first two years. The first to leave was due to pregnancy and this enabled Carly to connect to the alter of loving children and her own abuse related to this. This period was difficult as Carly engaged in more difficult topics; the staff were the ones who had to remain adult. This challenged the services. Carly also decided that her therapist was her mother and other staff were her sister and brother-in-law. Carly also noted that there were perpetrators watching her through the television and in her attic. Carly became quite paranoid and support was given by psychiatry to prescribe medication.

At times this period became unbearable and, for the manager of the service, the fear of what could happen was very high. The main concern was that if it became too unbearable Carly may need to be assessed under the Mental Health Act and potentially detained, and, knowing local services, this would be very detrimental to where Carly was emotionally. Through putting in additional support with therapy sessions being increased, reducing change and, at times, doubling up staff, they all managed to support and work together through this phase. Towards the end of it Carly decided to change her name again to an alter that "holds" them all together.

Additional management tools that enabled the service to survive

Throughout the three years the process of giving staff a place to debrief/offload to psychology enabled them to gain inner strength to cope with Carly. This can be difficult at times. Staff had the opportunity to receive one-to-one support with some attending individual therapy sessions to contain their own emotions in reaction to what was being discharged from Carly. The manager's role was to enable this facility by managing budgets. There are always additional costs incurred for staff support. This factor shows the need for a high cost placement, as the additional support can be hard to deliver. This can lead to a failure in the service if the right support is not provided, especially if strangers are brought in.

Staff need to be very boundaried and keep their own issues away from work. For a small staff team, working long hours, this can be hard. The staff supported each other and at times of crisis staff hours were altered to four-hour blocks due to the intensity of the service.

Staff had a company mobile phone they could utilise to access psychology, which enabled a "holding" system that emulated what Carly had. This all worked extremely well together.

With regard to commissioners during these years, the key outcome was reduced hospital admissions and Carly was quiet. The placement provides a high level of support but within this time period there was a significant reduction in episodes of self-harm, hospital admissions, and absconding. In fact they became almost non-existent. As staff assisted Carly to access other local services where there would once have been a crisis point, other staff who were trained could provide backup. This happened when Carly turned on the team leader of the service who, for her own safety, was removed from the service. This did cause issues; however, it was managed internally within the current contract and additional staff were enabled to take over. As time progressed Carly tolerated changes and more staff.

Current situation

At the time of writing, in thinking about the amalgam we have used, we are focusing on an average of five years since Carly moved to her bungalow in the community, with support from the same provider. The points at the beginning still remain. Carly has a stable environment to live in, and has worked with her staff team to decorate her home, and it has been adapted to meet her needs. Carly has had a stable staff team and has two key staff members plus a team leader she tolerates, and can express how she feels in times of distress. Carly has changed her psychologist, because of retirement, and continues to engage with the therapy process. Carly has remained with the support package and wishes to continue living in the community. Carly has enrolled with the Open University and has become a valued member of the local community.

Training

The staff team complete mandatory trauma-informed care training and at the current time fifty per cent of those working with Carly have continued this to a level five qualification. This has enabled them to understand the Frankish Model and implement this within the working environment. They "hold" Carly wherever "Carly" may be and try their best at all times to enable Carly to be more integrated and to live an ordinary valued life. The service is as good as it can be made at all times. Solutions are always sought, and rejection is never considered.

The main challenge for management

It may have already become clear but the main challenge will always be the appointment and supervision of appropriate staff. The individuals who do well are exceptionally mature and able to put others first. They are treasures to the service and to the care industry generally. The accidental training they have received from Carly has helped them in other services too so it has become a mutually supportive service. However, at times there will be issues of needing to appoint and train new people, and support everyone during the settling-in period. It is not possible to relax and there is constant change as the alters join and separate, come and go. There is no period of stability of any length of time, which makes life interesting, but also means that the need to pay attention is critical. In the TIC model this can be seen to be pre-individuation, which is of course the situation with DID, where the primary individuation process has been disrupted or destroyed by the traumatic dissociation. The support for staff to provide the secure emotional base is of paramount importance.

CHAPTER FIVE

Making progress

What is the day and what is the time?
How do I keep them all in line?
They do what they want and do it with ease
Without a thank you a yes or a please.
I lose lots of time and I have lots of fear
I wonder what happens when I am not here
Will you please tell me how I should cope
Because what they are doing has too
    much scope.

What are these flashes of memory I get?
What are they showing me and how do I let
Them come out with me knowing and
    finally have joy?
Are they a girl an animal or boy?
I am confused and I need to know
Who will come here next and who will show
What happened to us and what do they like
Or will they forever make me take a hike.

The host was so scared and at fifteen
This was the most horrid thing she had seen
She did not understand the alters that came
She felt oh so lost and like she was lame
She needed the healing therapy gave
It felt like conducting a musical stave
She needed the help and she needed it so
She would know more of what each
    did know.

The memories came for each of us and
The host had no idea of what was to hand
We all told our truths and healing began
Programmes also came and felt like
    forever ran
We became poorly and better again
And it was a cycle of hard work and then
It is still a trial but we now have strength
To carry on healing at a greater length.

The first time I knew of Carly was when I was asked to see her for assessment. I looked at the file and suggested that she needed to be assessed by an expert in DID. There are few sources of expert assessment in the UK and it is always valuable to have that assessment and recommendation in place. Other people with DID have also been offered services with the same model, as well as some with outpatient therapy only. The more complex the condition, the greater the need for the holistic approach. The report produced by the clinic gave the direction for therapy. Carly had been previously engaged in therapy with another person and this had helped her to accept the diagnosis of DID but had not really helped with processing what it meant or helped her to face the past trauma.

Initial sessions were with several different alters who all seemed to want to be known and accepted. All of them were welcomed and engaged with. Each had their own story to tell. They were many different ages, with a number of teenagers, and had varying degrees of traumatic memories. Some of them would draw and write. Others would talk. Some were silent but needing to be acknowledged. The pattern of several people coming to speak, or be present, became established and continued for the next years of therapy.

It became clear, from very early in therapy, that the different personalities had experienced extremes of trauma, and that they survived the horror by sharing it out between them. Some people may have had experience of therapy but this may not have been able to recognise the variety of selves. It became clear that they (the ones I met first) could trust me and that we would be able to work well. I made a commitment to work together for five years and this was achieved. Several support strategies were put in place for between sessions, like a goodnight text and email contact during the week. Later, sessions were increased to twice a week, one double session and one single session. It was a long and painful journey through the horrors of a childhood in a cult, with flashbacks and memories surfacing all the time, and hostile alters trying to work against recovery.

An excerpt from a poem written by a child alter:

They made me different, they made me wrong
Made me sing to their own song
And then they hurt me to the core
Until I just thought no more

Programmed alters

One phenomenon that became evident quite quickly, was that some alters had been generated in response to traumatic experiences, but some had been forced onto the host by torture and programming. Programming does, fortunately, seem to be fairly uncommon, but has a history with the works of a Dr Greenbaum and is written up in a paper by Hammond (1992). Carly had an alter calling himself Dr Green and he was very officious, always attempting to sabotage the therapy and the life of the host. The techniques used to establish "slave" alters include the use of electric shocks and other cruelties, as well as physical and emotional deprivation, amounting to abuse. As more and more stories came to light it became harder to understand how the authorities had not been aware, but then it became even more clear that the family had been part of the cult and therefore had deceived the relevant people who came to enquire about the child.

Accepting that there is traumatic reality regardless of distortion is a major part of the development of the therapeutic relationship. It is hard to accept that such dreadful things can be done by parents to their own children, or any children, but unless it is faced as possible, there is no future for the therapy. The horror has to be acknowledged and the pain shared if there is to be progress. The first months are about testing the therapist to see if they are strong enough to manage. Supervision is essential to help with the containment. It has been my experience also that there are always more stories of experiences waiting to be heard, more alters who have not felt brave or safe enough yet to speak out. Most people with DID have therapy twice a week and longer sessions than one hour. This enables other parts to come out. They may be shy or afraid and can only find the courage to surface if they are given enough time. This pattern of therapy has been established by the Clinic for Dissociative Studies (CDS) and was adopted locally to accommodate the seriousness of the condition.

Host alters

Early on in therapy with Carly, there was a dominant alter who acted as host for a few months and was able to prepare some written material describing some of the life experiences and the alters who had lived through specific times, giving ages to these alters. It was very helpful and those alters have maintained those ages throughout, not aging, but working through what happened to them, and some of them seeming to reach a level of peace. Some alters would come to therapy for a number of weeks and then go, which seemed to fit with some level of resolution.

An example of an issue like that might be of a young alter who reported being held upside down and threatened with being dropped on her head. The fear was palpable in the room and the trauma still as clear as if it was yesterday. This sort of trauma that has stayed with one part does not resolve naturally but becomes stuck in some part of the brain and stays there. Bringing it out into the open allows it to be talked about, tears shed, the pain of knowing the parent hated them faced, and eventually, some more mature acceptance that we can't choose our parents, but as adults we can live a different life.

Working with multiples

This becomes therapy with many people at the same time, as each part is a whole personality in themselves, and needs to be related to as such. It becomes possible to say "can Y come back please?" and this is usually an important thing to do at the end of the session, so that a competent adult alter can be there for when support staff return. Once the support staff have met the other parts this becomes less important, but generally it is good for the present host to know that the therapy session is finished.

As time went on it became clear that a very young alter had reported extreme fear in circumstances of death and murder. In a flashback in the therapy session a graphic description came, which was sickening to listen to. The fear was tangible as the re-living was experienced. The description of murder, blood, and ritual sacrifice was horrific, but there could be no doubt of the authenticity of the feelings. This alter has stayed as a core personality and carries the pain of the five- to six-year-old child. Her memories corresponded with her birth mother leaving the household and there remained confusion, for the therapist, about her role in the abuse and the cult. It was always made clear that the father and grandfather were implicated as cult members but the role of different women was not so clear, other than that they never provided a safe attachment figure, and were cruel in different ways. This led to questions about the survival of the individual in the face of such horror and the implication that there must have been at least one person who provided some nurture and love. Otherwise it would be expected that there would be serious psychotic illness. Dissociation is a defence that prevents psychotic breakdown but there still needs to be someone "good enough" for the personalities to survive. It became clear that this young alter had experienced some warmth from a neighbour who treated her with love and respect. This was undoubtedly an element that enabled her to survive.

Animal alters

As time went on a few animal alters also made themselves known. One of these was a protector and took responsibility for keeping the body safe from sharps and overdoses and suchlike. In the past there had been serious cutting and overdosing, as well as other forms of self-harm. A major part of the support has been around stopping self-harm and avoiding suicide attempts. The 24/7 support has been essential for this, as hostile alters are always on the lookout for opportunities to kill the host (see Negative alters, below).

The protector animal learned to work with the staff to keep everyone safe and there have been no serious incidents. There have been occasional instances of sharp objects being hidden, and items broken to make sharp edges, and some minor scratches, but that's all. Z is always quick to tell but also needs the recognition of her role. If support staff take it from her, it leaves her feeling useless and unwanted so there is always a balancing act to ensure that everyone is working together. The pattern became established of alters making themselves known in therapy, then, in time, agreeing to show themselves to support staff, or agreeing that the therapist could tell others that they were there. This has continued to work well.

There are other animal parts who have different roles, and represent some gentle parts of the self. One is very wise and can be relied upon to put things into perspective if others get lost. This includes the therapist! If something is not understood, K can be relied upon to let the therapist know by emailing an explanation after the session, or coming into the session to explain. What this also shows is the range of intellect and knowledge that is shared out between the parts, but doesn't necessarily exist in all parts. The therapist needs to be able to adjust to whomever they are speaking with, making sure that no offence is given or trust will be undermined. Some of the animals carry feelings of freedom and peace, so seem to have come into being to hold these positive feelings during the abuse in childhood.

Male alters in a female body

Most systems will have alters who are a different gender from the body and this can be very confusing for them. Especially if they are male but don't have a penis, and then have to cope with menstruation. Some of the male alters have suffered intensely from punishment as well, which seems to relate to the male oppressors, and their determination to humiliate and denigrate, perhaps because they see reflections of themselves. One male alter that I have worked with extensively, has been the one who has found it hardest to trust anyone, always expecting to be ignored and dismissed, with very low self-esteem. Helping him to face his anger and pain has been very challenging. He felt brave enough at one point to use the empty chair technique, where he spoke to an empty chair, imagining his abuser in the chair. The experience was very emotional and poignant and did help him to release some of the feelings, with some reduction in anxiety. But the pain is so intense that is can only be alleviated a little at a time. This alter remains very sensitive to any experience of rejection or perception of being ignored. There was a time when a previous therapist had referred to him as having succumbed to the Stockholm syndrome, and joined with the oppressors. He found this very insulting and the hurt lasted many years.

Negative alters

All DID systems have hostile alters and these can be very scary. People with DID and programming have an internal programmed system that is designed to kill them before they tell anyone about what has happened to them, or identified any abusers. Quite early on in therapy with Carly, a superior hostile alter came into the session to warn me off. It was male and very intelligent. The experience was like listening to a university professor telling me what to do, with a mental flexibility that could deal with any argument. This indicated that there was a high level of intellectual ability in the system and this has been shown to be so, over time, with the host alter being able to pursue higher education. This hostile alter has since moved over to the positive attachment side, after many altercations over a number of years. The process of moving from dark to light has been encouraged and facilitated wherever possible, with the emphasis on acceptance and forgiveness. There is recognition in the system that most of the dark parts came about through torture or with some need to defend the self, that none of them is inherently evil.

More alters

As therapy progresses more things come to light. One teenage alter had anorexia and at one time the whole system was being treated for this, although other parts could eat quite happily and not be ill. This was confusing for those who didn't understand until they became more able to communicate with each other. This was done partly through using a communication book, and partly through the therapist being able to explain to others what was going on. Eating remains a problem. Some eat one thing and not another and so on. This has been able to be more regulated by the presence of staff who can offer gentle help with food. This can lead to conflict but usually helps. Physical conditions that require the regulation of some foods are common in people with DID. This seems to relate to the fact that food and attachment are always linked, as they are in the primary relationship. Disturbed attachment always follows from living in a controlling cult and leads to attachment being a key factor in therapy. There has to be long-term therapy and patience in providing secure attachments to enable that therapy to be effective.

Roles in the cult

Another key feature of the life of a programmed person with DID is their role in the satanist cult and some of the young females are used as breeders from the age at which they can conceive, so often having their first child at thirteen and then every year after that. Some report being induced early so the average can be more than one a year. Experiencing flashbacks to induced births of dead babies, or babies that live for a short time, is gruelling but an essential part of the therapist role. Grief for the lost babies leads to depression and despair and a wish to die. This issue can be the focus of therapy for many years, with different alters who have had babies, or miscarriages, or induced abortions, or who think they have. Some of the memories are very stark, of the surroundings, the people present, the pain, and the blood. Most remember the baby being taken away and then being left alone, cold, and neglected, to look after themselves.

Linked to the need for babies is the extreme sexual molestation, being used as prostitutes from an early age, and ritual impregnations to conceive a baby for sacrifice at key dates like midsummer, Halloween, Christmas and some other dates that become significant for specific cults. The memories of young alters of being sexually used and abused are hard to listen to, but must be tolerated and processed if there is to be any resolution and progress towards accepting that it is over and won't happen again. This latter point is crucial and links to the need for the 24/7 support to provide that level of safety and trust that is needed. Issues that surface in therapy can't be suddenly forgotten and support staff may need to provide reassurance for many hours afterwards if there is to be therapeutic gain. The unconscious material would not surface if it wasn't safe to do so. The implication is that others with DID who only receive outpatient therapy may never address the deeper issues. Some can, but, if they do not have a safe place to be between therapy sessions, it is very difficult for them.

Developing trust and attachment

The transference within the therapeutic relationship is very strong and important. Where primary relationships have been so destructive, the work of therapy can be the development of secure attachments initially. It is only after the development of trust that the more distressing images and memories can be addressed. Sometimes the transference is so real, and the wish that the therapist was, in fact, the good parent, can lead to extreme behaviour at times. There was a very distressing period when Carly held this belief and told everyone that her name was the same as the therapist and that the therapist was her mother. This was worked through in therapy and tolerated by the outside world, eventually being recognised as a transference phenomenon. There was no rejection or anger from anyone and the acceptance of the desperate need to be loved and parented became part of the healing process. There were many tears during this period, and anger, but all extremes of emotion were accepted, there was no rejection, and in time the reality was recognised and accepted.

With such a complex psychological profile there will, inevitably be some alters who themselves have additional problems and paranoia has been one of those. Some alters live in fear of intrusion and attack and experience so much fear that it is at the level of psychosis. But it isn't true psychosis as other alters do not have the same experience. However there is benefit in prescribing medication for the symptoms in order to allow the system some peace. The consultant psychiatrist has been willing to prescribe where indicated and this has helped to alleviate some distress. The trust in the GP has increased as the GP has been able to listen and accept the complexity of the psyche and concentrate on the physical manifestations. As would be expected, the level of trauma leads to physical illness too, mainly joint and muscle pain and disability, as well as gynaecological issues. Mostly these things are addressed in therapy, work done to identify what is in need of physical intervention as well, and then taken to the GP.

More and more

One thing that has become clear and has to be accepted, is that the system can be so complex that, no matter how much progress is made to resolve one issue, another one will surface. There is always another programme, always more alters who need to work through their pain and distress. The other providers have clients who have had therapy for more than ten years, and, although this is more than most can expect from the NHS, they have been able to live useful lives and learn to control the extremes of responses to traumatic memories, so have been much less of a strain on other emergency and mental health services. It is possible to work quicker with the therapeutic support between sessions, but it is still a long road to recovery. Dissociation is a defence against pain and fear, and so the self becomes multiple. This will always be so, although some degree of integration is possible. It may be that living as a multiple and learning to look after all the selves, is the way forward for some. It is certainly important not to stress the need for integration as the purpose of therapy.

Involving the police

As the alters gather strength, they become able to voice their wish for the perpetrators to be found and punished. There will usually be a group of professionals as well who have missed identifying the abuse in childhood. The pain of recognising the neglect can be huge, and almost stronger than the anger at the perpetrators. This seems to be because the others should have been trustworthy so dishonesty or incompetence is added to the acts committed. Once sufficient memories have been expressed that involve risk, it becomes important for safeguarding to ask the police to investigate and we have found them willing to do this, and very helpful. Sadly, they can rarely find the information that is needed to substantiate the claims, as the tracks have been well covered over the years, and were kept from the victim at the time. Carly and other alters have very clear memories of places where abuse happened, but do not know where that place is geographically. They may know a town but no more. Or the place may not exist anymore. Records may not have been kept. It becomes very frustrating for all concerned and the fear of not being believed rises again. The local police were very helpful and positive in their interactions with Carly, but were not able to find evidence to support what she could remember, other than knowing that social services had been involved to some extent. Support via therapy was essential to facilitate the facing of the traumatic memories, the thoughts of failed parenting, and then the frustration of not being able to take legal action. This work continued for some months quite intensively and has continued to rise again from time to time.

Physical health

Health issues have been another avenue of therapeutic exploration and attention. Physical health is frequently affected by the trauma of the abuse and treatment can have been itself traumatic, making trust of health professionals difficult. Once settled in her new home we found an excellent GP who was open to understanding and learning. Sadly she moved and it took some time to build a relationship with the next one but this was achieved over time. With the GP support it became possible to face difficult gynaecological examination and then a referral to a consultant, with further examination under anaesthetic. As her therapist, I attended these appointments initially but, more recently, Carly has been able to attend them with the support of her trusted support staff.

The therapist role has been quite different from usual outpatient therapy, where people come along for sessions and generally manage to stay contained between sessions. The complexity and enormity of the issues when there are many personalities makes this containment virtually impossible. It increases with time and is an indicator of progress. The therapeutic support includes the individual sessions, at least twice a week and longer sessions during a crisis, plus some email and text contact, plus attending appointments with police and medical staff. It is not dissimilar to a parental role but can't be that. There has usually been no positive parenting so there is no experience of feeling parented. What develops is a trusting relationship between two adults, where the therapist begins to be able to trust that the person with DID will stay fairly contained between sessions, and the person with DID trusts that the therapist will be reliable, honest, available, and able to tolerate the horrific memories.

Resolution?

Over time, some of the alters seem to go quiet. It may be that their issues are resolved, or at least acknowledged as having happened and can't be changed, so are accepted. Some alters change as they have more exposure to the outside world and a therapeutic experience. These become stronger and gradually take more charge of the system, enabling a degree of ordinary life to become possible. Some maintain their role that they have always had, coming out when needed, staying in when not, but watchful to make sure that everything is safe. Sessions continue to have a variety of people attend, occasionally only one, with others listening but not speaking. Some sessions can have a range of different views from different alters about broadly the same event, but with each alter remembering only parts, it falls to the therapist to make a coherent whole and then check with each one that it reflects their experience. This can take weeks or months, and can change again when another alter comes forward later. There are some consistent themes and accounts, which indicate the severity of the trauma around those things. They stick in the mind of the therapist as well, so can usually be recognised if they come up again from another perspective. The most traumatic things, as would be the case with trauma for everyone, relate to extreme fear, especially in childhood, being controlled and neglected, and vivid imagery of violent incidents including blood and gore. The flashbacks can be very disturbing but do lead to some healing once they are out in the open and can be processed. It can take months to process some events, with many alters helping, and these require that the therapist can tolerate hearing about it, and seeing graphic drawings too.

Assessing progress

Progress in therapy can be difficult to assess. Measuring change in the incidence of calls to emergency services is one aspect. People with DID living unsupported make frequent visits to A&E and often use the mental health crisis team number to call for help. They reach a point where they cannot manage to stay contained and will sometimes engage in risky self-harm behaviour, cutting, taking overdoses, and suchlike. Sometimes this will be after reported having been accessed by the satanist cult, other times it will be to avoid being accessed. Unfortunately, all DID systems have some alters who will willingly go to the cult, and these can be "called out" by key words or phrases, so there is always a risk of this happening. If one alter sets off to meet the cult, another may surface on the journey and take evasive action to prevent the contact, but this can lead to other problems. So an alter who surfaces on public transport, not knowing where they are going, may try to get off the bus or train and put them in danger. An associated issue is money. One alter may be saving money for rent and another will spend it on taxis. Debt becomes a huge issue, with no clarity about who is managing what. Worry about money can come up in therapy sessions, as debts can lead to threats and fears for safety.

The main observable evidence of progress is the reduction and then cessation of self-harm and suicide attempts. Then better self-care and attention to diet and appearance, associated with care of the home environment. Better self-care includes managing diet, medication, and attendance at health check appointments. Another indicator is developing working relationships with support staff. As these improve with developing trust, it becomes more feasible to engage in a wider range of activities.

There is a close link between the availability of the intellect and anxiety. As anxiety reduces, the ability to think clearly increases. This can lead to the individuals being able to study and learn new material. DID uses an extreme amount of energy to keep the self together, creating masses of anxiety. The more relaxed everyone is inside, the more able they are to engage with outside. This facilitates the learning of new skills and can lead to engaging with higher education. The prospect of working in the longer term becomes viable and some people with DID have gone on to become therapists themselves, or to other work that uses their skills and experience.

The main factor, however, must come into the description of improved quality of life. Most people with DID lead chaotic frightened lives, subject to the horrors of repeated abuse in the context of rituals over which they have no control. Without therapy, or in the early stages, programmed alters take part willingly, leaving the others to suffer pain, confusion, self-loathing, and fear. A life lived in an ordinary house, doing ordinary things with the support of staff who are understanding, non-judgemental, and safe, enables the development of a secure sense of self that may be selves, but with an awareness of that, enabling each to trust the others and to live a shared life.

Another excerpt from a poem:

I am the one who went through hell
I am the one who can't tell it as well
I am the one who was not believed
I am safe to tell now and I am relieved.

CHAPTER SIX

Being support staff

Will you listen, will you hear,
We come to you with heightened fear,
We want to talk, we need to play
We need a better brightened day
We need you to fight for us
And to never make a fuss
Will you listen, will you care,
We so need you to just be there.

We cannot walk this path alone,
There's so much dark, and so much stone
Bad people are at every turn
And we need you to help us learn
Will you be the one that sees
Hear our cries and hear our pleas
If you are then all we need
Is to take the gauntlet and proceed.

This chapter has been woven together to give a flavour of what it is like to support someone with DID living in an ordinary house in the community. We work one to one, so there is always one of us there, but when there, we have to be the one who manages and keeps everything and everyone safe. None of us had worked with someone so complex before but we had worked for the employer so felt supported to do the work.

The words of one of us!

Meet Butterfly

Working with Butterfly was difficult at first as there were communication problems, as Butterfly did not speak. She would communicate with sign language as she did not have a voice, and she would sign very quickly and I could only understand a little bit of sign language myself, and those mainly the basic signs like how to ask for a drink or ask to use the toilet or ask for food. This was similar to work we do with people who use Makaton sign language.

So we needed to find a way that staff and Butterfly could communicate as this clearly was not working as staff could not understand her and she could not understand them. We found the best way was to use writing as a way of communicating and that worked better. Butterfly would write down what she wanted to say and staff would write a reply and the conversation problem was solved. But at times Butterfly would not communicate with staff for long periods of time. She would just sit at the computer and not communicate for hours at a time. This for me was a very lonely time; just sitting there in silence for hours was hard. You wanted the phone to ring or someone to visit just to have some sort of conversation. I think I found it hard working with this person: I could normally have three or four different alters a night and they were all really very chatty and this was what I was used to on a daily basis so to go from that to not having any communication was difficult.

What was even harder was trying to explain to people outside of work, people on the bus who would talk to her, the reason why all of a sudden the person they spoke to could not talk. We solved this problem by telling people in public that she had a really bad throat infection that was painful when she talked, so it was best not to talk. People seemed to accept that and sometimes staff would communicate for Butterfly when needed.

Shopping and paying the bills was difficult as Butterfly loved spending money and going round the shops. Every time Butterfly got the money she would go out and buy things for the others, and for herself, and over time she would buy less and less groceries. This slowly became noticed as sometimes at the end of the week there was not enough food to last and no money to get any more as all the money had been spent.

Also over time staff started to notice the bills were not being paid and reminders were coming by post but they would be hidden and when staff mentioned the bills they were just told that they have been paid when other staff were there. Over time staff noticed that the money and bills were getting out of hand and with staff and psychology input it became noticed that Butterfly needed help to manage the finances so a plan was made to help with this.

And Rosie

I will never forget the first time I met Rosie. I was sitting in the living room watching television with another alter when all of a sudden there was this big roar and it scared me, really made me jump, and then this really sweet little voice said: "Hi! Hi Rosie! I am a sneaky panther and I have something for you. Wait there, I will get it for you."

Rosie went to another room and came back with a knitting needle and gave it to me and told me not to be scared as Rosie found it and it's safe now. Rosie explained to me that "the hostile alters want to harm the body and make staff think that the body is going to hurt themselves so staff would want the body to go to hospital in a locked room because they are bad and don't deserve to live in a house and be happy and they should be locked away." These were her words, not mine. When this would happen, and it did on many occasions, Rosie would need lots of reassurance from staff that we believed she is not bad and that it was not her that wanted to hurt them. This would sometimes last all day. Rosie needed to constantly be reassured that she was believed and not a bad person. Sometimes this would lead to a dark alter coming out. The alter called himself Dr Green. He would tell staff things like "you know I am right and you don't believe the others. They are all bad and I am going to turn them all to stone and get rid of them all and I am going to hurt the body and they will go to prison where they belong." Sometimes you could ignore the hostile alter and they would just leave but on some occasions I would have to call Rosie out and she would come with a big roar and she would again need to be reassured that I know she is not a bad person and that the hostile ones are bad or do bad things. Of course I explained that she would not have survived without the dark alters and they would learn what had happened eventually.

I don't want this to sound unkind but sometimes it was hard for staff to have to constantly tell Rosie and other alters that you believed them, especially if something bad happened. Of course no one can believe everything somebody says—there is always distortion—but it matters when they ask if they are believed that we can agree that something horrid has obviously happened to them. It was hard constantly saying it over and over but I know how important it was for them to hear and it was important to them to know they are believed, especially by staff. At times like this it would be hard on staff and we needed to have psychology support. Just someone who understood what you were going though and you could talk to and not have to explain everything because they understood.

I'm not sure when but after a while staff were finding it difficult so it was decided for a while to cut the shifts short and instead of doing a full eight- or nine-hour shift for a while we did half-day shifts, four or five hours. This was just for a while until things got better.

And another voice

In my time spent with Carly there have been a few dominant alters. The first I met was Honey, who had an internal team to cope with the day-to-day tasks. Honey was quite shy and nervous but when she got to know you she became quite confident. Shaz was the main socialiser and was about the most in public. Then there was Cath who acted as an accountant paying all the bills and doing the paperwork. These three worked very well as a team until the hostile alters stepped up the internal abuse.

The hostile alters basically want the body dead until they can understand how they were made to be like that. As their strength grew, day-to-day tasks were not being done, and they would continuously try to make Carly self-harm. Their main objective was to get her to return to the abusers, but they didn't account for her staff team being strong and keeping her safe.

They couldn't get Carly to return to them so she was forced out of the body. Lottie and Leanne, who are twins, and are about ten years old, took over. As these new alters came to the surface, Carly's team also disappeared. This caused problems with the finances and the running of the house and this meant that appointees were then assigned. These twins suffered terribly with paranoia, which caused more turmoil inside and problems for the staff. The paranoid side of the mind told Lottie and Leanne that the staff were the abusers, which led Lottie and Leanne to believe they were unsafe.

They started to pack up treasured belongings that they gave to the therapist to remove from the house and look after. They permanently had an overnight bag packed and left near the door. They were also told that there were cameras in the house watching their every move. As a result their personal care suffered. They continuously got staff to check for cameras especially after trips out. They hated being in the house and spent hours going to the neighbouring cities visiting shops. This is when the appointees had to take more control. This is something the alters still struggle to cope with, as it shows they aren't as strong as they want to be.

Throughout this period of paranoia they felt that certain members of staff failed to meet their needs and they were forced to leave the team. This led to many changes in the staff team and the work rota. Which changed how we worked and forced a new dominant alter, Butterfly, who had no speech and communicated through sign language. This posed problems in the community and with friends with learning difficulties, as they could not comprehend why she could no longer speak. Butterfly was around for quite some time; her friends with learning difficulties were told of the illness of "Shaz". This pleased the dark alters as more people knew what was wrong.

Then we got Carly, and the hostile ones were quiet for a while. Carly came across as a very positive, confident young lady, nineteen years of age, who wanted to "start living, not just existing". She started to celebrate her birthday and her friends' birthdays. She even bought them presents and made them cakes. Christmas is also now celebrated with presents for all alters. This was a really big thing as these special occasions had always been linked to abuse. Carly has also found the strength to attend the Open University and is doing very well, although the hostile alters have tried to sabotage this, so a break in study was needed. She has also found the strength to start going on short breaks, but so far only with myself. The first was to a nearby city during a food festival. As this was a first, our trip was planned in detail so management and therapist knew where we should be at all times and remained in telephone contact throughout, Carly just with psychology, and myself with the full team. It was agreed that I was on shift 24/7 and shared a room with her. This was to ensure that the hostile alters could not make her flee back into the hands of the abusers. Most things were paid for in advance; spending money was heavily restricted and in my care, so we did not deviate from the plan. Whilst away, various alters came to enjoy the activities. The one that sticks in my mind was Esme in the Disney shop. It was like watching a child whose Christmases had all come at once, which in itself caused problems. Onlookers saw a thirty-something lady in a wheelchair but hear a seven-year-old little girl's voice with a passion for a certain character, which was great fun for us but very strange for onlookers to witness; mainly the adults, the youngsters were much more accepting.

On the last night we were away, the dark alters tried to sabotage pleasure found in the trip by trying to convince Carly that her home would be gone and I would be returning her to her abusers. Fortunately a telephone call with psychology calmed and reassured Carly. She was then able to enjoy the rest of the trip. We have now been away on other city breaks, shopping weekends, spa breaks, and to the seaside. As trust has developed between Carly, myself, and the support team, restrictions on the trips have lessened. Daily plans were not needed, Carly was in control of her own money, and I only had to text my team leader at the end of each day. Our activities have included visiting wildlife parks and zoos, going to the theatre, and other cultural events; we also experienced world cuisines, and Carly is now confident enough to go away with friends and a different staff member.

There are still many things that cause upset in Carly's life and daily hurdles to overcome. One that has been ongoing for about a year is a mind control programme that has activated the voices of certain abusers from the past. These remain internal and refuse to interact with staff. They are constant and they are exhausting to Carly, but she somehow finds the strength and energy to visit her friends and continue with her Open University degree. When she is down and struggling we remind her how far she has come and what she has achieved with her current support team around her.

Another staff member: knowing "Lady B" with her DID

Initially, I had heard about a lady who goes by different names and "personalities", but were indeed "alters" who came out randomly, sometimes a "protector" or "reporter" (by that I mean with a photographic memory) which can be called out by staff if needing guidance or help in any way. Sometimes this will or won't if staff felt a "dark one" was trying to harm Lady B's body (the host).

I didn't know much about DID when I started working with Lady B, but the internet provided some knowledge about multiple personality disorder (MPD). I asked Lady B to help me help her. I've always been honest and straight with her, and this has secured a good working relationship.

Over the past two years, we've laughed, cried, and sometimes got angry with happenings. I've drawn on my humour and strength to carry Lady B through her hard times.

We still laugh about the first time I experienced a "switch". We had been busy all day and after tea we were relaxing, I was sat in a chair reading, the TV was on low and Lady B was on her sofa. It was pretty quiet, when suddenly, "roar". I nearly jumped off the chair. An animal alter had decided to introduce herself as a young female but a cheeky one. This alter is a protector, and she will often tell us (staff) if any dark ones have got hold of anything that may harm the body. I'm adaptable and we both laughed. I've been privileged to meet a few in my time with Lady B, new ones and some that have been dormant.

A day in the life of a support worker is unpredictable and being able to adapt to a person, animal, child, or teenager of any sex or nationality is, I believe, a good characteristic.

I refer to DID as "having a time share apartment". Everyone lives in the host body, and pops out to share time with us—playing, writing, cooking, gardening, all different.

Another perspective from another staff member—my introduction to DID

My first experience of DID was as a member of bank staff covering sickness leave. I was asked if I would meet with a client and see if we were happy to work together. I must admit to being not only nervous but also very curious. Obviously I had heard of conditions that were described as involving multiple personalities, but had not had one-to-one experience of the condition.

The initial meeting went well and it was agreed that I would start to provide cover within the service. Suffice to say I went in as a temporary team member and remained to work full time within the service for the next eighteen months.

The provision of service was extremely complex. The aim was to provide a safe haven for our client; a place where she could be free from possible contact with past abusers and somewhere that she would eventually come to call her forever home. All this needed to be put in place along with providing care and support for the many different alters within the system.

The team consisted of five main members of staff providing twenty-four hour support. The aim initially was to allow our client's many alters to feel able to make themselves known to staff and to begin to build a new life in a safe environment. At times this was extremely difficult as the system consisted of alters whose main role was to fragment the team and allow exposure to past abusers. It was vital in those early days that the team remained strong and supported each other through what was a very difficult and emotionally draining period. Staff felt able to call upon each other, to talk through difficulties and plan further strategies to ensure continuity of care.

To say there were difficult and challenging times would be an understatement. As alters grew in confidence, the disclosures of historic abuse became more prolific. Staff support was underpinned by twice-weekly therapy sessions for the client and a weekly feedback session for staff. This allowed psychology to protect the integrity of their sessions, but also allowed staff to feed back concerns and gain a better understanding of the service provision.

Over time the team produced a service that allowed the client to remain safe but was flexible enough to deal with the many facets presented by the client and the internal systems.

During my eighteen months as a support worker, I encountered many different alters and also several hosts. (The body will have a prominent person within the system who will present as the main host for a period of time.) Initially the team remained constant, but then a crisis caused a fracture within the team and the need to introduce new members.

Changing role to managing a service

It was at this point that I took on the role of managing the service and the team. This in itself led to some initial problems as I was no longer perceived by the client as a member of the team, but as someone who had moved on and now occupied a different role. There was definitely a form of what felt like resentment towards my new position; however, this could also have been seen as abandonment. I had for the past eighteen months worked at the centre of her service and was now moving into a position of having to consider other clients and staff teams.

The role of managing the service, preparing the rota, and providing the staff team with regular support and supervision is not without its difficulties. Following the crisis within the system, supporting the client became even more challenging. Staff were under a constant barrage from alters from both the dark and light side of the system. There appeared to be a continuing battle to disrupt the team and destroy the safe environment that had been created. There was a need for constant vigilance from the staff team as sharps were hidden and attempts were made to store medication in order to attempt self-harm. It was at this point, and following guidance, that the decision was made to reduce the shifts from eight hours to four hourly. This was done so staff would be able to tolerate the level of distress our client was experiencing. However this did have a somewhat negative effect on the client. She had been used to having staff for long periods of time and had used this to spend hours away from home either shopping or just wandering around with staff. The impact of shorter shifts now meant that staff and client needed to return home in order to carry out staff handover. This was met with resentment and at times anger. As the manager and in effect the person who created the rota, it was more often than not aimed at myself.

I soon realised that I had two vital roles to fulfil. First, I needed to ensure that the staff team were given adequate support so that they could work effectively within the service. This was done by the use of communication books to pass on concerns to other team members, regular team meetings at which staff could discuss ways of working and share good practice, and, most importantly, the provision of a psychologist with whom staff could just talk about how they were feeling. The latter proved to be vital in ensuring staff felt mentally strong and able to tolerate and validate the feelings and expressions of distress that were displayed by the client.

The second part of my role was to establish a working relationship between myself and the client. There were times when I needed to take a firm stance in order to prevent things from spiralling out of control. Planned shopping trips were often cancelled if the alter present was displaying behaviours that would put the body at risk. This resulted in verbal abuse from the current alter but eventually a realisation that it was done in order to keep everyone safe.

Holiday and sickness cover also presented us with its own set of problems. The introduction of a new member of staff into the team was almost always met with anxiety and distrust. Staff would need to be introduced gradually and shadow shifts with trusted team members were essential. It was also important that the existing members of the team reassured our client that all was okay and that she would not be put at risk. It takes a particular kind of person to work within this service. Many staff cannot understand or comprehend the level of support required, whilst others feel unable to commit to a service that requires such emotional input.

There is also the need to justify the provision of such an intensive service to funders. Like many people they may never have come across such a condition and may well struggle to understand the complexities surrounding it.

The needs of the client are ever changing; at times it appears we take one step forward and then two steps back. However, the provision of service works. The client has moved from being isolated, persecuted, and abused to living in a community that welcomes her. Over the past few years we have celebrated birthdays (something that she never felt worthy of or able to do in the past) planned trips and taken holidays supported by her staff, and made plans for the future. To the outsider it may appear far from perfect but the amount of dedication and commitment displayed by an amazing staff team has made a huge difference to her life.

To summarise, my constant fallback position to both staff and client is that the service is both unique and bespoke and what we do makes a huge difference.

CHAPTER SEVEN

A client's voice

Do you get why we need help
Do you really care
Do you understand our need
And can you be there
Do you see that we aren't safe
Do you understand
Why we need to get away
They are underhand.

So many may not get abuse
Accessing and the like
But we know you do and need your aid
And ask for your hand to strike
Please make us safe and hear our cry
We know that you are able
And thank you in advance of this
For making us all stable.

"Creating meaningful lives". This is the motto of the company that took over our care. Holistic and trauma-informed care are at the heart of our supporters, and therapeutic attachments are very important to them all. They took us as we are, and accepted us, right from day one. They became involved in every aspect of our lives, no matter how trivial it seemed. Staff were trained in the principles of disability psychotherapy, which made them easier to talk to. This is the basis for the title of this chapter.

To say things became different is an understatement. The application of funding, therefore giving us staff support, meant that suddenly we were launched into a life with staff there twenty-four hours a day. As for me, the then host, it was very confusing to start with. Actually, everything I was trying to take care of in life became the responsibility of others who we did not know and if I am honest I was a bit unsure of it at first. I felt confused and hurt as, at fifteen, I thought I should be able to handle everything, but could not. Having staff there, however, felt a big relief too, as all those threats that we had on our life were finally stopped from happening, and we could finally breathe easy. It felt much more peaceful as well knowing that this was the case—we could finally sleep knowing we would not be killed in our bed, as we had been threatened.

There were still many doubts in our mind as to whether the staff were safe, but they each eventually proved themselves to be so. Gradually we became involved in the world of care plans and risk assessments to keep us safe. I came to be relieved by these, as people inside did do things to put us at risk as well as outside people, and it was a great weight off my teenage shoulders. It seemed like it was safe, and we were assured of a forever home, but to actually believe it took a lot. We could not believe the kindness of people in finding us such a peaceful place that was to become our safe haven.

It was very different living within the constraints of risk assessments and care plans but they were much needed. Every time something came up the coordinator of our care wrote a new care plan, all with the aim of keeping us safe. Some inside disliked them with a vengeance because they put perceived limitations on them, but I, as host, knew they were very much a good thing. Staff took over a lot of the running of our daily life, and some alters thought it was wrong, but the internal fight was worth it. Safety protocols, such as staff having our keys to stop them being locked out or in, were put in place, as was assistance with cooking and many other things. I was just relieved to have the help and support to keep us safe.

One example of a safety protocol put in to keep us protected, was a paper form for if unsafe people were seen. This was for monitoring purposes, and made us feel safer, as if anyone was spotted repeatedly following us, staff would know and would act accordingly. This made us feel calmer and cared for in a way you cannot describe. It also gave staff the opportunity to log unsafe people, and see who was following us, so that evidence could be presented to the authorities if needed.

Something else that was closely monitored at this time, and to a lesser extent now, was our use of the computer. This was because we had alters that were still in touch with people from the coven. We were also receiving suspect emails that had strange coven-related information contained within them. S, the then host, was terrified, and staff had to constantly reassure her that by printing them off as evidence for Dr Pat Frankish she was doing the correct thing.

Another thing that was taken over by staff was the administration and monitoring of our medication. Because of programming and our general suicidal tendencies, as well as not taking needed medication, we were becoming very unwell, especially since we are diabetic and were not taking our insulin. With staff support and watching us take our meds, we were able to get back on track with them. At one stage, we even had to show our tongue to prove the meds were taken, and although now this is not done, they are still very much observed and signed for by staff. Staff also attend medical appointments with us, and know all about our medical conditions. This is helpful as it enables us to know what has gone on if we switch and do not remember appointments. There is also a diary kept by staff for appointments in case we forget when they are, or someone dark inside tears up the letter.

We were placed in a community of people who all embraced us with a care that we had never known. From the moment that we first met them all, they were so considerate towards us that we wondered if we deserved it. One lady within the community, and one gentleman in particular, were so good to us on our first day, that they have to be mentioned, as we have never been treated with such loveliness by people we have never met before. It was nerve wracking knowing we were going to meet all these people at first, but they soon put us at our ease.

We were scared that we would not be accepted by people, but they took us just as we are. They wanted to know us and had no intention of hurting us. The staff were accepting and took us as intelligent human beings. We were finally wanted and accepted by people who really cared about us.

Even our new friends cared enough to hug us and be welcoming despite not knowing us too well. We were finally safe.

The immediate community around us were also briefed on the fact that we had people inside of us that may come out sometimes. So, if a little one came out with a higher pitched voice than our "normal" voice, they accepted it with good nature and humour. Most of all they never batted an eyelid, and just readily accepted whoever came along.

The times when we had the little children in our system out playing with staff or having a hug were special. Knowing that they had time to actually play and have the time to just be themselves meant the world to them and me, and the fact that they were in safe hands to do so did us all the world of good. Safe play was and is important to them, and with the staff factored in, it gave and gives them the chance to learn to become the kids they are now. The babies in our system had the most benefit of all, as all the care they did not get when the body was their age, was given to them then. I remember coming back after one of the babies had been very confused, as a staff member was talking to a baby and I did not remember! It was disconcerting in one way and yet, oh so good at the same time knowing everyone was finally getting what they needed.

Even as a fifteen year old you need to play and have fun. I benefitted greatly from playing games such as Scrabble and Monopoly with staff, which enabled me to just act my age instead of doing the boring adult stuff which is part of being host of a DID system. Finally I could just be me.

There were times that staff were confronted with little ones mainly who did not know where they were. According to a staff member, one young girl alter of ours came out, very confused because there was no grass hill outside the window. She was then told where she was, and shown around the house, and this and the fact there were toys to play with soothed her and she left happy. Although she was rarely seen afterwards, she obviously knew that she was safe, and could finally rest easy. This is one example of our staff working hand in hand with our system, to show everyone how different things were and are now.

There is one person in our system, also, that must be paid tribute to. She was very badly hurt physically, and because of this is profoundly disabled. This is because of a bad beating she received at the hands of her abusers. She can only talk via blinking, but through her internal carers has a voice. Through them talking in therapy and drawing her portrait to show how she was after her attack, she has been able to cry, and have her pain felt which, of course, is important for everyone. As the famous humanistic psychologists Carl Rogers and Abraham Maslow argue, it is important that people's emotional needs are met as well as their physical ones. Dr Pat Frankish said that she represented our most disabled parts and as such was vital to the system. We will always be thankful for her contribution to keeping our system alive, despite her trauma and terror.

A further alter in the system with a disability, Broken, was around hosting the body for a number of months. She is unable to speak, and had to conduct conversations on paper or computer with staff, which was most frustrating for her and she used to get angry sometimes. Her emotional state was also a cause for concern and frustration, and staff had a number of occasions where they had to ask for support to understand and handle Broken. She did not understand the world around her very well, and because she did not talk, it made activities of daily living even harder. It was still a life though, and this helped Broken tremendously and she grew as an alter, through therapy.

The one thing about DID is that you never know whom may be hosting next. You may, for example, go to bed or be doing something, and a totally different alter takes over, and then may stay and become host. This was the case with Broken and myself. There have been a number of hosts all with differing abilities in our system at different times, and none of them has been able to do activities of daily living; for example, you could not expect a young child to do food shopping and it be healthy!

We finally had a life. We could even do shopping in the daytime with help, and feel safe in the care of staff. The funding given to us gave us a life we had never ever had. We could finally go out wherever we wanted and do what we wanted, and know that we were totally safe, in whatever we were doing. We will always be grateful to the funders of our support for keeping us safe, as we have a life now that we would never have had without them. Especially, we would thank the chief executive of the funding organisation for his care, consideration, and input towards our case. He fought for us and supported us like no official had done before.

We also acquired financial appointees from our support work company, which helped us with our finances no end. Due to dark alters literally throwing money away and tearing it up, as they did not want us to use it, we ended up with hardly anything at all. We also did not know how to manage money in terms of bills, and as a new nineteen-year-old host I had never done this before, and therefore needed help and support to keep our system on an even keel. We are indebted to Dr Pat Frankish, Amanda Brock, and their office manager and staff team for helping us to take care of ourselves financially.

Gradually over time, we were able to do many things including even going to a gynaecologist to gather evidence of our abuse, under general anaesthetic. This was done with the support of the coordinator of our care and was very helpful to this end but also to remove a piece of glass put there by abusers. Had we not had the support of Dr Pat Frankish and staff we would never have been able to do this scary procedure.

There were and are also times of year and anniversaries in our life that represented and represent a triggering time to us, one example being Halloween. Times of year like this are awful because they remind us of atrocities that happened to us. Things in the shops and media, in fact in most places, advertise and sell these commercial events not even knowing what they are doing to some people. At these times going out becomes difficult, but staff reassured and supported us to get through these horrible times, using their skills and simple tender care.

Colours were and are also a trigger to us. Red, black, white and purple in particular are bad for us because they remind us of blood that was shed and satanic robes. Staff combated this by not wearing the colours that affect us, and at the same time we have worked on these colours in therapy. This has helped, to a small extent, to desensitise us to these shades, and now we can tolerate them a little better. The impact they have on us, though, is that we cannot wear these colours and they sometimes hurt to see them.

All the time our staff were helping us, we were also receiving psychological therapy, for the wounds the abuse and mind control had caused and continue to cause. This has been a long drawn out process, and still continues. The body memories, mind memories, and flash-backs have been terrible to work through but we are getting there, slowly, working with Dr Pat Frankish and, more recently, Dr Natalie Cross as well. The hardest point to grasp at times has been that for ther-apy to work properly it takes time, and there is no quick fix, and that sometimes it involves going backwards to come forwards, if that makes sense. The therapy has also been augmented by support from our staff post-sessions, by them just being there for us if we are crying or in need of a hug. This has been much needed and welcome at times, and totally different to the therapy we were given where people did not understand our DID.

Psychology support also provided a text message and email service to us and our staff. This meant that Dr Pat Frankish could keep up with where alters were at as they needed to communicate, but it also meant that staff could text Pat if they had any problems as well. This was a most helpful and needed service, as things such as programming problems and traumatic episodes could be dealt with at the time, and reassurance provided to ease the situation. This was follow-on work that the editors have provided to people who were still in grave danger.

Hugs have been very important therapeutic interventions for us. [Staff note: Touch is a very sensitive delicate issue in therapy and social care and great thought has to go into what is safe and will aid the client.] The family we grew up in never hugged us or wanted us, and with the sexual abuse memories we have also, we were not used to real safe positive touch. This made even a pat on the arm scary to be given to us. The hugs we were and are given as part of the therapy process really helped us to feel wanted and cared for which we were not used to. This is something we will always be grateful for as well, because it has taught us that not all touch is for a sexual reason, and is just in fact safe positive touch, as when we first arrived we were very wary of this.

One message, translated, means that one of our little alters feels much safer than she did before moving, and having staff around make her feel much better. The safety element is so important for the little ones, because they are so scared all of the time, and need space to play and just be the children that they are. It is also important for the little ones to have staff members with them when they have bad memories. E also wanted people to know that staff make E's life nicer, which says so much after what she went through.

Alters like Cath also had needs met in a very special way. Cath is deaf and used British Sign Language to communicate with staff but they did not understand it. What was put in place instead, was that staff wrote to Cath and she then responded to them. This was a long-winded way of doing things for some people, but they persevered and Cath really came out of her shell. She was our internal administrator for a long time and really helped staff understand computer communications, and yet she is a lot of fun as well. We do not know if Cath will ever regain her hearing through therapy, but we are hoping that one day this may be possible. She is a wonderful person, and it would be wonderful if this could happen.

In our previous chapter we described Kaz and her issues with food, anorexia and bulimia. We have done a lot of work with Kaz, in therapy and with staff and now she rarely throws up and no longer has access to laxatives. Kaz still gets triggered and obsessed about food and dieting websites, but she is working on making healthier choices with food and telling staff if she has urges to make herself be sick. We have seen through therapy that we became big in one period, partly from baby weight, and partly from not wanting to look attractive to men so they would not sexually abuse us. The same issues fuelled anorexia. This is a large piece of therapeutic work to undertake, but we are gradually trying to work together to eat less unhealthy foods, and hopefully, one day we will be much healthier than we ever have been before.

> I used to want to be really big to put the customers off me, but it only served to turn some on instead. I still persisted though and when I was pregnant this got even worse. Now though, I want to learn to stop the binges and urges to throw up and get better. It will take time, but I have to believe I will get there in the end. Eating disorders are hard to get through and win over, but I am determined to get there one day.

Staff were very patient with our darker alters too. Every so often a dark one would come out and be verbally aggressive and not that nice to staff. They also told E, a little child alter, that her favourite cuddly toy was going to be taken away, and tried to convince her staff were people they were not, who E did not even know anyway. This is just the product of their abuse, however, which they used by the process of transference and projection to put on others in our system. These times were not easy to handle for all concerned and embarrassing for me as host to come back and find they had been making mischief and havoc. Staff, however, developed protocols and put care plans and risk assessments in place to stop any undesirable behaviour in its tracks. The thing we are most grateful for is that staff persevered with them, as we expected them to give up on the dark ones, and now they are much more internalised than they previously were. Dr Pat Frankish described it as the last flick of the tail of the dragons from them, and we very much hope this proves to be the case.

I used to be dark, and I would do everything I could to obstruct the healing that was taking place. I would try to mess with programmes, I would threaten the little ones in the system, and I would be verbally nasty to anyone who got in my wake. The reason was that my abuse left me cynical about trusting human beings and people perceived to be a threat, including safe people. I was also scared of other dark people inside higher up the hierarchy than me. I was fighting against my very existence though, and it took Dr Valerie Sinason to really accept me and tell me I was wanted for me to break down in tears, and want to be accepted by the rest of the system.

Over time, with Dr Pat Frankish by our side, we did a training session for staff on living with DID, in which we included some of the poems we had written at that time. Pat introduced some newer staff to how to work with us, and people said it was helpful to them. It also did a lot to validate us because we had never had the opportunity to actually train anyone about our condition, especially given the fact that people like us just don't get that opportunity.

We also were able to start an Open University course in psychology, with staff and psychological support. This has enabled us to understand our selves, behaviour, and triggers a lot more, as it means that we are able to have a grounding in psychological theory. Having a theoretical base to start from has enabled us to deal with abuse memories as they came up related to the course. One example of this was Milgram's (1963) shock study, which brought back memories of being shocked in the nether regions; following psychological support for this issue, we were able to do an essay on the study and got a good grade.

Learning new things is something we are very passionate about. It is the foundation of understanding and growth particularly emotionally and knowledge wise. Being given the opportunity to start again as a mature student is something we take seriously, even though as host I am only nineteen years of age. Really it gives me the chance to do what I never got the chance to do when the body was my age.

We have had the opportunity to go on holiday with staff several times. This is a time of therapeutic bonding in that you get to know staff better. Breaks brought relaxation and the chance to be ourselves and let our hair down. It also enabled us to go to places that had been unsafe and see them in a new light as staff were there to keep us safe. They are also good fun and allow us to just be our own ages in a safe environment. Later this year, we are even going on a group holiday with the community of people we live as part of, which although different to one-to-one breaks, sounds like great fun to us!

A blow to our system came when our long-term therapist retired from our care team. Programming took over, relating to her retirement, and the grief we felt at the first solid therapeutic attachment being severed was very severe. At times we could not speak without crying and thinking about the lost attachment. It was like grieving after a death, even though we knew that she had not died. She had dealt with everything for us, including training staff in our condition, and we suddenly felt very alone. We were angry with her at the same time, and hurt for her leaving us in the lurch. Knowing that a therapist is going to retire one day is one thing, but the shock still comes when you reach the day it happens. We had a resistance to change, and have trouble trusting new people because of our abuse, and so when the new therapist became involved with our case, we were very nervous. Our abusers had a no talk rule about the abuse, and whilst this had evolved with our previous therapist, it started again with Natalie. She put us at our ease, however, and showed us that we can talk about whatever we want to quite safely, and that we don't have to worry about not being believed, which is important to us. Alters are now beginning to talk again, which is something that we never thought we would be able to do. This shows us that trust is becoming a little easier, which to us, is a little progress.

Five years of therapy later, and four years of safety have done us no end of good. We now know that we can go to staff with problems and they will not judge us. The therapeutic attachments we have meant that we can tell our staff if we see someone unsafe, without fear of reprisal, and when hard times come we weather it together. If unsafe people arise, they are recorded, and our mind put at ease. We are developing a friendship with a neighbour, which is something our staff are helping to foster, and we are beginning to feel part of community life. Most of all, we are safe to just be us. We have a situation currently where an alter wants to bring back a self-harmer, and staff are dealing with the situation by removing bleach and all sharps, but this is only done as needed. The little ones feel safer and continue to talk and play as they need to, and things are far from peaceful, but they are in no way as bad as they could be. We are still not safe to be alone yet, but we are working on it.

Our new psychologist works in a very different way, and focuses on play and music as forms of therapy in sessions. She has already taught one little alter who did not know how to play, how to begin having fun, which is something that she has never had the opportunity to do. She also promotes much play with our staff and they have benefited from it greatly, as have I as host, because it gives me some much needed down time. Rest is important for me, and when the little ones play or have a story read to them, it gives me the time to sleep inside a little.

As for music, it is a very therapeutic measure to use. Our new therapist has assisted us to feel the trauma in our body through the use of music, by listening to it, and describing how the music makes us feel inside our body. We talk of an episode of a particular television programme where there are piles of rubbish making hills under the carpet. This is how we describe our complex post-traumatic stress disorder in terms of avoiding it. Every time we listen to music and feel the associated feelings, we take a little bit of the rubbish out of the carpet, and start to look at the memories the music has brought up. The use of a drum has even given Butterfly, a previously mentioned alter that cannot speak, a scream by banging the drum hard and loudly.

One hindrance to not being alone is what we will call "the others". These internal programmed people constantly goad us 24/7, and have for months on end, and seem to be the sceptics in our system. They do not even believe in DID, and are constantly blinkered and in denial about it. They want us to harm the body again, but we are stronger, and with staff by our side we are unable to do anything anyway. There are four of them and they represent blackmailers and bad people, from the past, and one day we may report who they represent, but for now, we have enough to cope with, dealing with the internal versions. These representations are now trying to undo everything that was and is being done in therapy by bringing back the programming we had previously, in the hope of ultimately ending our life. Dr Natalie Cross, however, has reminded us of the power of attachment-based therapy, and that with our staff and psychology team around us we can get through anything. Even if they activate any internal people to try and hurt the body, our team provide a holding environment, and in that we are safe. It is just so very isolating to be consumed by an ever-present programme.

There have been many revelations about the others in therapy recently, and it seems that they are playing mind games, which include trying to turn us against our staff team and psychologist. This is something that other inside people have tried to do with varying degrees of success, and very much draws on the issue of trust, and the others have worked on this tirelessly. For anyone who is trying to work with people with darker alters, constant reassurance can be needed and emotional security in staff, or a whole team can break down. Also, there is a need for staff to be extra vigilant with what they say, as one thing can hurt and set us, and others with DID, back.

One of the hardest things to cope with in our experience is staff team changes. It is so hard to trust new members of staff, because of what we have been through, and any new members of staff are met with a lot of worry and fear. What many people did not realise was that what we needed and indeed need is a consistent small staff team with whom we can engage and build therapeutic relationships, which has at times been handled with varying degrees of success. At one time, when we were unwell, we had a very large staff team, and this was dangerous to us because we could not engage with anyone because they were not around long enough. This was detrimental to our healing and hampered our growth at the time, we believe. Now, however, lessons have been learnt, and we have a smaller team, which is much more supportive and safe, and enables us to live our life despite our limitations.

Now, there are not as many care plans and risk assessments as there were, and some things are on a more even footing. We still have dark alters, but they are internal, and therefore staff do not see them. It is still noisy inside as always, but we are learning to try to handle these misguided inside people with staff support, and to put them to rights. Overall, though, the important thing now is that we are stronger with staff by our side. It is still at times a very bumpy ride but staff give us hope of one day having a real future. Hope was never anything we had before, but now we know that one day, in time, we may be able to spend a little time alone, and get even stronger within ourselves. It all takes time, but we know that we will get there one day. Most of all, we are learning to fight the darkness that was and can be our life, and trying to find a new and enriched beginning.

To anyone who would like to work with someone like us, there are a few simple rules to follow and you will be just fine. Firstly, do not be judgemental, and just take us as we are. We have seen atrocities you can't even imagine, and as such, need simple tender care and a sense of belonging. Don't try to be over zealous in what you do, but always remember to be there for us, even if that means from a little distance to start with. Please don't be dictatorial in what you do, and think on the fact that DID can be seen as a coping strategy of intelligence. Also, just remember that we can't control what other alters do, as they have their own thoughts and tastes. Finally take us as people, and not just laboratory cases to be studied, and then we will take you as you are too, and you will be accepted.

CHAPTER EIGHT

A new therapist

A new life starts, the old one ends
Its time for staff and real new friends
A spot to be, a safe new space
A private and a quietened place
Somewhere where we can be us
Without folks making a real fuss
A place where whatever happens we
Are unquestionably safe and free.

A place where care and support abounds
No more evil sights and sounds
We have a freedom never had
A real reason to be glad
No more sadness, no more fear
Just happiness forever here
A place to work on issues and
Walk the path both hand in hand.

Introduction

A feature of long-term holistic therapy is that when, for whatever reason, a therapist leaves, Amara Care has to find a new therapist. This is very complex and we thought it would be helpful to provide a sample of the early stages of a new therapist relationship, using an amalgam again. This is written in the therapist's words.

Before I begin describing a short, but hopefully to be a long and successful, journey, I will provide a brief explanation of the terms I will be using in this chapter. Carly is currently the host and so predominantly present; the other alters are referred to by Carly as the "system", and this is how I will refer to them in this chapter. Because Carly and her system are many, I will often refer to the collective as "them" unless I am describing a specific alter, in which case I will refer to them as him/her as appropriate. The system are supported in a 24-hour specialist support service that ensures they have a member of staff with them at all times; in this chapter I will refer to the staff collectively as "the team".

I began working with Carly and her system nearly a year before her previous therapist was due to retire. We had already met a few times within the local client community. Seeing how well loved Carly was by the community, I was looking forward to getting to know her and the system better. I was immediately stuck by how welcoming Carly was of me; Carly has an incredibly warm heart and a desire to help others. It was clear that she had a number of apprehensions about my skills working with DID but encouraged our relationship by providing literature relating to DID and, more bravely, information that related to the system personally.

The system

Quite soon after starting our work I was visited by Rosie, whose role it is to ensure that outside others and the system are safe. Rosie is part of a group within the system that are represented by animals and birds, who are incredibly spiritual beings. Rosie is an eight-year-old black panther whose entire life has been dedicated to finding, frankly, genius ways of hiding objects that could do harm to the body. This has been dangerous for her in the past but she continues to take this role seriously. Rosie is incredibly playful (I should note that her surprise entries where she roars loudly have made me jump from my chair on a number of occasions, followed by tears of laughter). Rosie delights in praise from others when successful in hiding dangerous objects (usually sharps) and a good game of hungry hippos (which she usually wins). Rosie's courage allowed her to engage with me quickly and soon provided reassurance to others in the system that I was safe and non-abusive.

Soon after, a number of other alters made themselves known to me. Each time I met someone new I noticed a deep feeling of honour mixed with delight that would lead me to teary eyes. This indicated to me the strength and courage that was required for them to do this. I was initially very worried that I would offend the system by missing when switches occurred, or even misidentify who was present with me. I was honest about this, and the system have continued to be patient with me, letting me know when switches occur and providing signals to look out for; I think I'm getting better at this but I'm sure the system would be a better judge of that.

I have already met so many courageous members of the vast system, which comprises babies, children, teenagers, and adults. Some alters are frequently present and take a strong role in maintaining safety emotionally and physically. S, for instance, is an alter who has been instrumental in bringing the system and body away from danger in the past; she continues to hold this role and will be one of the first to let me know when things are unacceptable or triggering to them.

There is a strong mix of personalities within the system. There are a number of highly intelligent and philosophical alters, such as Joshua and Carly, who help the system to work through some difficult challenges and programmes; there is also a great deal of creativity both musically, and with the written language (M, for example, is a talented poet). This can at times, for those who do not know the system well, mask some of the more vulnerable alters who desperately cling to life despite strongly wishing to end it; often these are very young children with big responsibilities (such as S who holds the switch for the self-destruct programme). Similarly there are alters in the system that are programmed and who continue to wish the system to kill the body or return it to the abusers. As such, mental capacity within the system is variable and extra care is needed from their team and the authorities to ensure decisions are made in their best interests.

It remains both a challenge but I think also delight for Carly, to meet everyone's needs within the system. Carly takes extreme care to decorate and furnish her home to ensure all within the system's likes are catered for; this includes having to consider clothing that would suit the needs of the males within the system. A, for example, is a teenage boy within the system; he can present to others as very strong and forceful, but in fact has a vulnerability which at its core comes from the need to be unconditionally loved and accepted. As he has held a protector role within the system for a long time this need can be missed. As such the system is extra mindful at times to consider his emotional needs. Recently this has been demonstrated by purchasing a football top of his favourite team (to the despair of some females), which has brought him much delight.

The needs of the system not only include likes and dislikes but physical ability and communication needs. Some within the system are either unable to hear completely or have been traumatised to not be able to speak, or even so badly hurt that they can only blink. Others in the system will try to aid the team to communicate but ultimately it is our responsibility to find ways of communicating and supporting emotional expression, such as writing, some basic sign language, music, and crafts.

As time progresses, more alters within the system are feeling safe enough to come and talk with me. Some wish to share their trauma memories and others enjoy exploring their likes and how these can be facilitated (for example purchasing of craft material or ensuring age appropriate toys are easily available). For those who have been away for some time, their needs can include orientating to time and also coming to terms with the fact they are now in a safe location, or that their relationship with their previous therapist has now changed and they now have a new therapist.

Working with such a vast system can mean that I am often providing group therapy. Although there is only one alter communicating and using the body at once, there are often others listening or commenting, and the developing co-awareness between a number of alters in the system can allow me to communicate to a number at once and also allow others to pass comments for the current host to communicate with me. It is not surprising, then, that principles associated with leading group analysts, such as Yalom and Leszcz (2005), of promoting attachments within groups to work through trauma and develop healthy relationships, are appropriate in the work, and complement the main theoretical approach, trauma-informed care, described later in this chapter.

From the outset of our work together, Carly and the system have been tormented by a programme designed to undo the hard work they had done before. This programme is referred to by the system as "the others". This programme involves programmed alters. The actual words the others use tend to rotate but the theme is always the same, to destroy the system's trust in the relationships made, to re-enact abusive ways from the past, and to deny the system's truths about the abuse suffered. Although they often feel like they are drowning under their power and influence, the system has shown itself to be incredibly robust—a testament to the strong relationships they have developed with each other in the system. In the face of the torment, the system will reach out to each other, support each other, and validate their experiences.

Using trauma-informed care

The trauma-informed care (TIC) model (Frankish, 2015) is at the centre of our work together. Of a number of theorists that are fundamental to the approach, the work of Bowlby and Winnicott describing attachment and "good enough" parenting inform the basic grounding for the therapeutic relationship. A great deal of work had already been completed prior to me starting with Carly and her system. Core safety had been established with her "home for life" and a core team that she trusts to keep her safe. This meant that I was taking over at a time when a number of alters had developed a great deal of insight and understanding about their DID.

From the outset it has been the aim to provide consistency and reliability to the system. We have our sessions at the same day and time each week and on the days that I am "out of sorts" I will acknowledge this so that they don't need to worry or try to figure out why I am different (their life experiences will immediately lead them to think it is for reasons relating to threat).

This is not always easy, however, when it leads to distress. For example, due to my personal circumstances I was unable to provide a reliable out-of-hours phone support that has been part of the support provided previously. This was a major blow to Carly and the system who experienced this as abandonment. There have been a number of occasions that my emotional response to their distress has made me want to rescind this, but I know that it would lead to inconsistency and inadequacy on my part, and so I have had to bear "the intolerable" for the system's best interests. This has continued to be difficult for them, but I think they mostly see that this is not an indication of a lack of care on my part but rather a difficult decision that is in the best interests of our therapeutic relationship.

Although I am not always able to respond out of office hours, I continue to provide both text and email support, which I respond to at my earliest availability. The aim of this is to provide emotional support and also demonstrate that I do not disappear between sessions and that I continue to exist; although Carly and the system will be consciously able to know this, unconsciously their experience of insecure and abusive relationships will have taught them that others are unreliable and may indeed never return. Rather than relying on me solely, the system is developing confidence at contacting others within the service who may be able to help, such as the domiciliary care service regarding team issues.

The system have been working with a core team for a number of years and have now developed secure attachments that allow the system to trust them to support them with frightening tasks such as cooking and attending medical appointments. There are members of the team that they will trust enough to share some difficult memories when they become overwhelmed and will hand sharps to them when found by R. The ability to attach to more than one person, other than the therapist, is a significant sign of the progress the system has made, and the dedication of the team who follow the TIC model.

A number of alters in the system have developed relationships secure enough to be able to internalise them. As such they are able to imagine what they would say at difficult times and take comfort in this; the most significant internalisation being that of the previous therapist. As described above, the system is currently experiencing "the others" programme designed to undo these secure attachments (this manifests as alters); as such, the team, the previous therapist, and I often come under "attack" by these alters. The secure attachments, however, allow the system to feel secure in the knowledge that they (the others) are lying and will reject their claims of neglect and abandonment, although this sometimes needs support.

Valarie Sinason writes about the pain of difference, which is one concept considered significant within the TIC model. For Carly and her system, this is often seen in the pain of difference in terms of family. It is deeply painful for them that the parents and family that should have cared for them cruelly abused them. Although they take plea-sure in their relationships with their team and service users in the local community, they are very aware that this is not a typical family. Particu-larly at times of year associated with family, they feel this pain of dif-ference. Our work both validates this pain and allows space to process this loss but also considers that close relationships do not always reside within family units.

The TIC approach in terms of individual therapy is fundamentally a psychodynamic one. As well as the therapeutic relationship pro-viding a secure attachment and safe base described by Bowlby (1988) and Winnicott (1973), it acknowledges that all individuals have an inner world, and that dynamics seen in the "here and now" hold their origins in past relationships, and the related traumas are often held in the unconscious to maintain psychological safety. The role of therapy in this regard has been to bring the unconscious into the conscious so that it can be worked with and lose its influence over their lives. Given the nature of the trauma, care is required to ensure all work is con-ducted within their "window of tolerance". That is, exploring enough to uncover significant issues to work with but not to such a degree that it causes the system to be overwhelmed. Some in the system are emo-tionally developed to a degree that they are able to explore more deeply than others; for example, a number of spiritual alters in the system are able to quickly spot parallels between the others' ways of attempting to distress the system and the ways in which they were abused. Some alters are more vulnerable to the others and find it difficult to challenge them, and require support to recognise the care that is provided to them, and their worth to those around them as well as to the rest of the system.

The influence of PTSD and trauma

As well as battling through DID-related programmes, Carly and her sys-tem also have the challenge of living with post-traumatic stress disorder (PTSD) or, as it is often termed, complex PTSD (due to the longstanding nature of trauma at the hands of those who should have cared for her). On a daily basis this creates difficulty in relation to threat perception, hypervigilance, and overwhelming emotions. Of particular difficulty are situations that replicate a sense of feeling uncared for, as in the past this has meant danger. Unexpected change, or indeed any change that is being caused by outside others, can create a feeling of fear and danger. For example, anyone who has had involvement in the care sector will appreciate how understaffed services can be; this often leads to changes in rotas. Carly and her system find this very difficult to tolerate, and the response by some in the system can be perceived by others as hostile; however, this is PTSD in action, and feelings of fear overwhelm them. When we are anxious we do what we can to alleviate the anxiety as quickly as possible, when we can't "run away" then we try to change others in whatever way we can.

Conflict can also be seen in the challenge of wanting to build an independent, fulfilling life, whilst managing the fear of being seen as "better" than they feel. Pressures on services, and constant cuts within the care sector, mean that the threat of reduced services is never far away. For Carly this creates an added pressure as she fears her achievements will cloud others' ability to see the deep fear and distress that still exists, which of course is at different stages for all of the alters. Their ultimate fear, understandably, is that if the service is cut too soon, dark alters or the abusers would re-access or potentially fatally harm the body. It can be easy to forget that it is the presence of the staff providing core safety that supports the system to make their achievements.

Carly and her system presented me once with a wonderful analogy of their trauma—they described their trauma being piled under the carpet, but it being so full that it always threatens to spill out, and often does. Our work often talks about which bits of trauma we want to take out from the carpet for us to process. But of course it is important to note that the alters have different things under their carpets, and do not always process at the same time. This means that the work can take a long time, and of course what style works for one, will not work for another. Similar to this, is different alters' abilities to work with emotion. Those readers familiar with trauma work will understand the significance of this, and those familiar with working with complex trauma will understand how challenging it is for clients to access, understand, and name their emotions. This is particularly difficult for Carly and her system who have a "no-speak" rule that we are constantly challenging. This does mean, however, that we can get creative, which is always fun.

Their trauma also has an impact on their basic needs. Food has been a significant part of the system's abuse. This has led to mixed relationships with food within the system. Some in the system cannot tolerate food and have had to work hard to overcome bulimia, while others' emotional states can lead to consuming quantities of sugary food that put their health at risk (due to diabetes). This has been a longstanding difficulty and it is to their credit that they have worked hard with this.

In therapy they have been able to explore their relationships with food and consider the function of this. Through this insight they have made gradual and sustainable changes to their eating habits that promote health but also allow for enjoyment of treats in such a way that does not lead to feelings of punishment.

Finally I will comment on "triggers". In PTSD different situations and sensory experiences often trigger intense trauma-related emotions and physical sensations. This is also the case in DID. Of note are colours; Carly and her system have colours that were associated with their abuse. Initially Carly and the system were completely avoidant of these colours, as they instigated too much distress to tolerate. Over time, they have been able to build new associations with colours, such as linking them with activities and staff they are safe with.

Getting creative

In order to access emotions, engage with alters with different needs, and to communicate, we have become creative in our work. A tool we have found to be particularly effective at accessing emotions is the use of music. Over the course of a few weeks, Carly and others in her system were able to develop a soundtrack to their lives. This included songs that represented significant times in their lives including fear, trauma, making progress, and hope for the future. They were then able to share this with members of their team to support their understanding of the systems' complex emotional world.

Some in the system are unable to talk or hear, or are developmentally so young that they can only interact at a very sensory level. As such we have used music again, to help communicate ideas. We have also used multimedia resources to help me learn a little sign language, and used drums to communicate different feelings and allow those who cannot speak to shout! For the very little ones, we have introduced age-appropriate sensory materials to encourage them to come out, so that they can have their emotions labelled and held, as they should have been, when the body was that age.

Over time the system has developed some degree of co-awareness with non-dark alters. Although this is a positive step, it can cause some sadness as they wish they could fully interact with each other; in fact a number of them share specific experiences (such as loss of significant others) and would benefit from peer support. To encourage this, Carly and her system have a notebook. Its initial purpose was to capture events between sessions for me to read, but in a very positive step has increasingly become a space for alters to share ideas, and offer one another support.

The future

The main aim of any attachment-based therapy, such as the TIC model, is to provide an attachment but then ultimately detach, as would happen in typical development. This is the case for Carly and her system too. However, in order to detach from a primary relationship, there is the need for a wider system of relationships to be available. Carly has already made a significant step in welcoming me into the team following the retirement of her previous therapist and long-term therapy (five years). Carly has been able to transition from a relationship of primary attachment to one that better replicates that of an adult parent-child relationship, that is, to know that her previous therapist is still available but she does not need her to hold all her distress. This is emotionally age appropriate.

In our therapeutic relationship, Carly and her system have gone to great lengths to welcome me. They have provided literature, and shown me great patience as I have come to learn more about DID and how to transfer my previous experience of working with complex PTSD. It reflects their significant progress that they have been able to tolerate my fallibility and indeed explore their needs with me and the ways in which I have not met them at times. For example, I am still learning how to spot when switches to some alters occur, and they support me by letting me know. When distressed, they are becoming more confident at letting me know when I have missed them and then discussing how I could spot them in the future.

At the root of all such occurrences of course is trauma and fear. Again in keeping with their progress, Carly was quickly able to trust that I would not intentionally harm them, which has allowed us to work in a more open way. To support this, Carly, the system, and I work with emotional honesty. Emotional honesty is not about disclosing personal information but being honest about emotional experiences. Life has taught them that when others are "different" the threat must be coming. It would be disingenuous not to acknowledge this and leads to fear that there is a malicious reason for this. By modelling emotional honesty, this is encouraging Carly and her system to do the same.

By supporting broader relationship development, and emotional honesty, the aim is that this will create safety beyond the primary relationships and support emotional development. Carly and the system's courage allow them to continue to do this in the face of years of life experiences that have shown them not to trust anyone or to have permission to feel any emotion; this and the work continues.

Work on processing trauma, as described above, will continue along with broadening emotional experience and creating this as a safe experience. Specific work continues too, such as reducing the triggering power of things like colours by creating new associations, just like we are aiming to create new experiences of relationships to replace the old and provide new attachment figures that the system can internalise to provide positive self-image, and helpful coping strategies to draw upon.

As mentioned previously, threats of cuts to services are never far away. The future for Carly and her system will inevitably involve this going forward. The responsibility of her team is to ensure that Carly and her system feel empowered and capable of having a voice, and that their team act as an advocate. It is essential that clients are heard and are truly collaborative in the process of deciding how their service should change in their best interest. All too regularly decisions are made by professionals that leave clients feeling powerless, frightened, and vulnerable. This could not be more of a risk for those who have been traumatised by those who should have cared for them. Without collaboration, this parallel with the past is quickly triggered and any trust can be easily lost, leading to the risk of self-harm, or re-access to abusers.

The world of clinical psychology is an ever-increasing cognitive behavioural therapy (CBT) one, whether that be traditional CBT or its successors such as dialectical behaviour therapy. These treatments are sometimes cited in guidance for working with trauma and there are some who would consider this to be appropriate for clients with DID. My very simple response to this would be "which one do you want me to do this with?" In DID there are numbers of alters all at different stages of recovery, all requiring a person-centred approach. Throughout my experience working in trauma it has always been clear to me that if the trauma is as a result of insecure and abusive early relationships by those who should have cared for them, then what is needed is a new experience of a primary relationship. As psychologists our job is to integrate our breadth of knowledge and experience to our clients' needs, not to force them into a neat, predetermined "care package". This battle continues.

CHAPTER NINE

Conclusion

There are voices in the brain
Making us feel quite insane
They try to trick, they try to boast
And make us look like fools the most
We need you to help us try make sense
We feel like we're behind a fence
So tall we cant get over it
We feel like we're not worth their spit.

We fight and tell them we're the truth
But think they might be in their youth
Is a programme in the frame
Or do these people have a name
They do not listen, do not care
Just make us know that they are there
We want to sleep but cannot too
Because they are not in our crew.

We want to tell them they are wrong
That they are like a pied pipers song
Following others in the dark
Without the light, no divine spark
Please help us know just how to work
With them until they cannot shirk
Their responsibilities
And work with us in total ease.

"Will you listen, will you hear?" writes an alter. It is a crucial question. We all need some level of dissociation to survive the ups and downs of ordinary life. Taking account of extreme cumulative trauma in another or oneself requires an extra openness that can lead to secondary traumatisation if we do not have adequate filters and support. Not everyone can listen let alone hear. Clients tell us very clearly the difference between listening and hearing. Yet even to try to listen is sometimes an achievement. "You will only hear half of it and you won't believe it," said one woman with a mild intellectual disability (Morris, 1994) to her psychotherapist who clearly showed the highest level of emotional intelligence.

Hearing the psychic narrative of a "singleton" is hard enough. What is the impact of hearing multiple traumatic narratives coming from one body? It is not surprising that the diagnosis of dissociative identity disorder changed its name from multiple personality disorder. As those of us in the intellectual disability field have always known, linguistic changes are prompted by a psychological process of euphemism—something that happens when the subject is not bearable and there is a wish to change the word to eradicate its toxicity (or example, from mental handicap to intellectual disability).

It is not surprising that professionals in the intellectual disability field have been prominent in the UK in recognising the nature, impact, and aetiology of dissociative disorders: see, for example, Bicknell (1994), Corbett (2016), Frankish (2015), and Kahr (2007). We have learned from experience that to the most vulnerable and chronically disabled the worst things happen, including ritualistic and organised criminal abuse. Indeed, when *Treating Survivors of Satanist Abuse* was published in 1994 with chapters by more than thirty clinicians as well as organisations like Childline, we were proud that Professor Joan Bicknell, the first professor of intellectual disability, had written in it, "both children and young adults with learning difficulties are at risk of ritualistic abuse. Our own sense of revulsion that this could happen may, through the mechanism of denial, leave our clients all the more vulnerable." (Bicknell, 1994)

We also learned that police, lawyers, judges, and educators, despite improvements, take longest to make the reasonable adjustments needed to ensure equal help for vulnerable victims. Former Detective Chief Inspector Clive Driscoll and Amara Care's local police are shining examples of good practice.

In 1979, when I first joined the pioneering psychoanalytic "subnormality" workshop (the correct word at the time) created by psychoanalyst Neville Symington at the Tavistock Clinic in London, my father, the late Professor Stanley S. Segal OBE had succeeded in influencing both Plowden and Warnock of the need for the inclusion into education of children with disabilities rather than keeping them in hospital.

Coming out of the army at the end of the war and entering the teaching profession my father was shocked at the E stream teachers given to the E stream schools and the conditions children with disabilities faced. He set about transforming schools into warm homely places, banning corporal punishment, educating teachers, and welcoming parents. Every summer holiday he and my mother ran a Jewish branch of the Children's Country Holiday Fund, providing children from the East End, who had never experienced a holiday, with a time by the sea in Sussex. In being true to their wish as deprived but loved children of immigrants, they wanted to give something back. My brother and I often thought they were at their happiest and I learned from an early age that both my parents longed to provide holistic twenty-four-hour healing environments to aid the most deprived and disabled.

When my parents moved to Ravenswood village, described by my father as "an island of sanity surrounded by a sea of madness", in the late 1960s, which offered lifelong village life for children and adults with an intellectual disability, I could see how much this kind of provision was missing from mainstream care. They would regularly explain how unfair it was to expect a worn-out parent to be able to provide the same twenty-four-hour care a well-trained staff group could. In running a village that welcomed parents but provided small "house groups" to promote attachments they finally considered the best all-round service could be offered.

At the same time Dr Pat Frankish had been living in the grounds of the former Caistor Hospital where her parents worked. She took in the benefits of understanding a holistic response in the same inherited way! Her father was the hospital manager and her mother was a ward sister. It was only when we finally met in 1985, after a northern psychoanalytic disability group was formed with Professor Nigel Beail that we realised what similar experiences and attitudes we had and how they had informed our disability awareness, despite our different cultural and religious backgrounds. Together with likeminded colleagues we faced the high level of abuse disclosures our patients brought to us and researched and wrote about this.

It was only when I began working with children and adults with dissociative disorders in the 1990s and recognised the disorganised attachments and early abuse that appeared to have led to the dissociation that I realised the enormous lack of provision at any level. If it takes a village to raise a child it also takes a village to break one. The deliberate attack on the minds of small children leading to dissociative identity disorder was an appalling sight to see and more so in a climate that, at that point, could not recognise the level of abuse, the involvement of female abusers, organised abuse, or organised abuse that also involved family members.

Whilst in the twenty-first century colleagues and I have worked with children and adults reporting ritual abuse from ranges of belief or pseudo-belief backgrounds, at the start of this work, in the 1990s, the most terrified children and adults reported a history of satanist abuse. Interestingly, linguistically, the small but vociferous number who could not face this subject or had discrediting agendas about it persistently used the term "satanic abuse", conjuring up a B movie Dennis Wheatley picture to aid denial and scapegoating processes.

We do not call abuse by a Priest "god abuse" and yet the term "satanic" was a ploy to bring in a supernatural term to avoid the all-too-common banal criminal reality. Interestingly, the term "satanic abuse" was first coined and deliberately used by special forces in the Irish troubles to try to invoke something that could cause disturbance. Satanism itself is a legal belief system in the UK and you can be a serving officer in the Royal Navy as a satanist as well as require your religious items in prison. There are satanists who would never hurt anyone and religious figures from every major denomination who do but it is interesting that despite stating this clearly in all talks and books there is a deliberate disinformation process to try to imply all satanists are being accused of abuse. Indeed, in one radio show in the 1990s I suggested the whole country should convert to satanism as it seems that Jews, Christians and Muslims abuse their children and satanists are the only people who don't, hoping humour could find a way into this curious national blind-spot.

In the period up until 1998 when I worked with the subject of ritual abuse and dissociation at the Tavistock and Portman NHS trust I became aware of the lack of safe twenty-four-hour places. Dr Kingsley Norton

(1994), then Director of the Henderson Hospital, one of the few therapeutic NHS hospitals, made clear that the group therapy culture that was the core of Henderson treatment did not work for such survivors as their accounts traumatised the rest of the group, and, equally, being in a group traumatised them. People with DID are, of course, living in a group all the time which is why psychotherapy without other external people works best. The Arbours Community Crisis Centre was prepared to offer respite but had mixed views about DID, and the libertarian approach of not locking the front door meant there was no twenty-four-hour safety as some states could be "called out" to leave and be re-abused. Nevertheless the therapeutic nature of the culture was welcomed and it was a national loss when it closed. The Retreat at York has also provided helpful grounding and a safe culture. A very small number of patients were lucky enough to have an understanding local psychiatrist who would allow them to self-admit on nights of perceived danger to them. However, most, even if they had a friend, partner, or parent who cared about them, felt in profound danger as well as at their highest suicidal level at the lack of a refuge. Sadly, in our experience, psychiatric hospitals have not been experienced as a refuge and some of the worst self-injuries have taken place within them.

"The operation was a success but the patient died" is a motto for the way risk-averse, manualised, non-bespoke treatments are endorsed at times of national insecurity. Professional teams might feel contained if the patient is hospitalised, but not the patient, or rather, rarely in this field. Within the USA Dr Sandra Bloom (2013) produced a model of a sanctuary but this did not spread to the UK.

When the Tavistock and Portman NHS trust transferred patients from the end of the research project Dr Robert Hale and I were involved in, to me privately, in 1998, the Clinic for Dissociative Studies was started. As the founder director from 1998 until December 2016 when, aged 70, I clinically retired and Dr Rachel Thomas became CEO, I witnessed over and over the damage caused by the lack of suitable training and provision.

Dr Pat Frankish and Deborah Briggs, successive chairs of the Paracelsus Trust, a charity to support DID patients at the Clinic for Dissociative Studies (CDS) set up by our first patron, Pearl King, a former president of the British Psychoanalytic Society, carefully looked into this subject. Whilst they found a safe room that could be offered on a bad night we found that a room without a trained carer could not help as most people we encountered would be too vulnerable to travel and stay on their own at a difficult time. The Paracelsus Trust commissioned Dr Alan Corbett to look into provision. Like Dr Kingsley Norton a decade earlier he found that it would be counter-productive to try to fund a specialised residential unit for DID alone as the nature of childhood experiences made being with other people with DID very problematic, more so than with other conditions. Alan Corbett tragically died in 2016 at the age of 51. His luminous last work has been published by Karnac.

CDS attempted to provide virtual therapeutic communities for one by adopting a team approach with intermittent weekly support. However, the lack of safe living provision was only too noticeable. A chance meeting at a conference with one of the truly nice members of NICE, Professor Pete Tyrer, revealed his major innovation of nidotherapy (2002). Although it was introduced for patients with severe mental illness, who had failed to respond to conventional treatments and were usually antagonistic to services, it was extended to other groups. The revolutionary aim of nidotherapy is not to change the person in a direct way but to create a better fit between the environment (in all its forms) and the patient. As a consequence the patient may improve not a direct result of treatment but because a more harmonious relationship has been created with the environment. The environment becomes the core healing agent.

However, another answer showed itself as already available and in existence. It had been hiding in plain sight. As a founder member of the Institute for Psychotherapy and Disability, the UK organisation started in 2000 for supporting training in disability therapy, I was well aware of Dr Frankish's many initiatives. In addition to providing the first-ever accredited disability therapy training in the UK, Dr Frankish provided homes for people with disabilities and complex needs. These were not "residential units" or "residential homes" or "homes" on a psychiatric hospital ground, but real lifelong homes with the client as the real official tenant. In other words, the client was matched with a suitable home of their own and Dr Frankish provided home carers, who were trained, and visiting psychologists, but the client had the tenancy, not a hospital or mental health trust.

These homes were not next door to each other but tenants were aware of the existence of other tenants who lived in their own houses. Some of the tenants with complex disorders who had an intellectual disability also had dissociative disorders. It was therefore a small step to enlarge the window of hospitality.

Having provided an onsite psychoanalytic assessment of several tenants with disability and dissociation it was a moving step to provide the same for tenants with a dissociative disorder, including people who formed part of the amalgam offered here. With a local team of psychologists and psychotherapists, assessments are full and rigorous: to gain NHS or social service funding this is crucial.

I was moved to be allowed to provide an assessment in the person's own tenancy. Each person I met was so proud to have a home that legally was their own tenancy. The specially selected and trained carers took great pride in aiding the tenant with the decoration and style of their choice, however unlike their own tastes it was! This was a rare experience for most, akin to having their own voice heard and respected in therapy. In providing some training for the home carers I was also moved by their commitment as well as their honesty about the secondary traumatisation dangers, as well as other problems that came from this specialist work.

On my last visit I suggested the staff should take the nature of this innovative work seriously and write about it for the professional journals or for a book. I did not expect the idea to crystallise at the speed it did with Dr Pat Frankish encouraging it now her book on the Frankish training was out.

Whilst there are survivors who come forward and write accounts of what has happened in their life to help others, many of these are understandably anonymous. There are also survivor-professionals who write from their professional context and need the freedom to not have to disclose their lived experience. Whilst the climate continues to be unsafe, although more understanding than twenty years ago, there is more impetus for therapists and others to speak the unwanted message to the rest of society. This is especially true when the subject includes belief systems. It matters all the more that there are publishers willing to deal with this subject.

Oliver Rathbone at Karnac Books received the Joan Coleman Award, presented by Orit Badouk-Epstein of the Paracelsus Trust, for courage and understanding in aiding the inclusion of this subject. Karnac has not only published *Ritual Abuse and Mind Control* (Badouk-Epstein, Wingfield Schwartz, & Schwartz, 2011) but also *Living with the Reality of Dissociative Identity Disorder: Campaigning Voices* (Bowlby & Briggs, 2014), as well as books on mind control and ritual abuse by Alison Miller (2011) and Wendy Hoffman (2014, 2016), and *Shattered but Unbroken: Voices of Triumph and Testimony* (Van der Merwe & Sinason, 2016).

Speaking about hurt within a religious or pseudo-religious context can evoke fears of being seen as illiberal and intolerant. There is also the deep fear of threats coming from fundamentalists of all belief systems, let alone members of groups who hurt others. These fears affect all sections of society, including police, publishers, and politicians.

I consider it helpful to make clear that I am not talking about any religion per se—only the human representation of it. I am particularly talking about attachment patterns. Those with a secure attachment to their religion (as to their family, nationality, place of work) are able to speak confidently about the positives and negatives of their experiences. It is those with a disorganised attachment who will fight to the death for the honour of a maltreating parent, representation of a deity, or religious representative. As one wise religious leader told me, "It is a sin of pride to think you have to fight for God's honour—you are implying He does not have the power to stand up for Himself." This is of course endemic to a disorganised attachment.

In a 2009 conference at the Bowlby Centre, in looking at change over the previous twenty years, I examined the way obedience, hierarchy, and professionals fearing for their jobs had tried to cause a silencing over this subject. Today I see the same processes. Additionally, with the huge discrepancy between numbers of people with all the clinical hallmarks of trauma on their minds and bodies and those whose traumatic experiences have been proven in court, we can see the pressure on risk-averse trainings seeking accreditation to disavow and dissociate any validity from the unproven. Despite the small numbers with a fictitious disorder, or Munchausen's syndrome, or deliberate intent to pursue false accusations, the equally small numbers of mainly non-clinical "false memory" proponents will continue their non-scientific pressure. This is not in any way to advocate an idea that all disclosures are accurate. With drugs and deliberate disinformation good officers find accurate memory living alongside distortions. However, by and large, people know what they have experienced and the whole of human communication is based on accepting people's narrative until proven otherwise. As I have said on many occasions (Van der Merwe & Sinason, 2016), if a woman comes crying to a walk-in centre that her mother has just died, the receptionist does not say in a cold tone, "I see, and this woman, who you say is your mother, do you have her death certificate and your birth certificate?" Our organisations need to be alert to silencing pressures that are against the best interest of clients.

And meanwhile, more and more people are coming forward, such as Carly and all who make up her amalgam. And one day they will write their own articles and books like this one.

"Will you be the one that sees
Hear our cries and hear our pleas
If you are then all we need
Is to take the gauntlet and proceed."

REFERENCES

American Psychiatric Association. (2013). *Diagnostic and statistical manual of mental disorders* (5th ed.). Washington, DC: APA.

Aquarone, R., & Hughes, W. (2005). The history of dissociation and trauma in the UK and its impact on treatment. In: G. F. Rhoades & V. Sar (Eds), *Trauma and dissociation in a cross-cultural perspective; not just a North American phenomenon* (pp. 305–322). New York: Haworth.

Badouk-Epstein, O., Wingfield Schwartz, R., & Schwartz, J. (2011). *Ritual Abuse And Mind Control: The Manipulation Of Attachment Needs*. London: Karnac.

Bicknell, J. (1994). Learning disability and ritualistic child abuse. In: V. Sinason (Ed.), *Treating Survivors of Satanist Abuse* (p. 152). London: Routledge.

Bloom, S. (2013). *Creating Sanctuary: Towards the Evolution of Sane Societies*. London: Routledge.

Bowlby, J. (1979). On knowing what you are supposed not to know and feeling what you are not supposed to feel. *Canadian Journal of Psychiatry*, 24: 403–408.

Bowlby, J. (1988). *A Secure Base*. London: Routledge.

Bowlby, X., & Briggs, D. (2014). *Living with the Reality of Dissociative Identity Disorder: Campaigning Voices*. London: Karnac.

Brand, B., & McEwan, L. (2016). Editorial: Ethical standards, truths and lies. *Journal of Trauma and Dissociation*, 17(3): 259–266.

Cheit, R. E. (2014). *The Witch-Hunt Narrative*. Oxford: Oxford University Press.

Edwards, H. (2005). *Faith, Religion and Safeguarding*. NSPCC internal briefing paper; revised 2007.

Fonagy, P., & Target, M. (1995). Dissociation and trauma, current opinion. *Psychiatry, 8*: 111–116.

Frankish, P. (2013). Measuring the emotional development of adults with ID. *Advances in Mental Health and Intellectual Disabilities, 7*(5): 272–276.

Frankish, P. (2015). Disability Psychotherapy: an Innovative Approach to Trauma-Informed Care. London: Karnac.

Gabbard, G. (2005). *Psychodynamic Psychiatry in Clinical Practice*. Washington, DC: American Psychiatric Publishing.

Hammond, C. (1992, June). Hypnosis in MPD: Ritual Abuse [Greenbaum speech]. Lecture at the Fourth Annual Eastern Regional Conference on Abuse and Multiple Personality, Alexandria, VA.

Hoffman, W. (2014). *The Enslaved Queen: a Memoir of Electricity and Mind Control*. London: Karnac.

Hoffman, W. (2016). *White Witch in a Black Robe: a True Story about Criminal Mind Control*. London: Karnac.

IS (2006). Believe. *Rainbows End—Support and Information Newsletter of First Person Plural, 6*: 4–5.

Kahr, B. (2007). The infanticidal attachment. *Attachment, New Directions in Psychotherapy and Relational Psychoanalysis, 1*(2): 117–132.

Liotti, G. (1995). Disorganised/disorientated attachment in the psychotherapy of the dissociative disorders. In: S. Goldberg, R. Muir, & J. Kerr (Eds), *Attachment Theory: Social, Developmental and Clinical Perspectives* (pp. 343–363). Hillsdale, NJ; Analytic.

Mahler, M., Pine, F., & Bergman, A. (2000). The Psychological Birth of the Human Infant. New York: Basic.

Main, M., & Hesse, E. (1990). Parents' unresolved traumatic experiences are related to infant disorganized attachment status: is frightened or frightening parental behavior the linking mechanism? In: M. Greenberg, D. Cicchetti, & E. M. Cummings (Eds.), *Attachment in the preschool years* (pp. 161–182). Chicago, IL: University of Chicago Press.

McQueen, D., Kennedy, R., Itzin, C., Sinason, V., & Maxted F. (2008). *Psychoanalytic Psychotherapy after Child Abuse: The Treatment of Adults and Children who have Experienced Sexual Abuse, Violence, and Neglect in Childhood*. Karnac, 2008.

Milgram, S. (1963). Behavioral study of obedience. *Journal of Abnormal and Social Psychology, 67*: 371–378.

Miller, A. (2011). *Healing the Unimaginable: Treating Ritual Abuse and Mind Control*. London: Karnac.

Morris, S. (1994). You will only hear half of it and you won't believe it. In: V. Sinason (Ed.), *Treating Survivors of Satanist Abuse* (pp. 159–163). London: Routledge.

Morton, J. (2012). Memory and the dissociative brain. In: V. Sinason (Ed.), *Trauma, Dissociation and Multiplicity: Working on Identity and Selves* (pp. 65–79). London: Routledge.

Nijenhuis, E. R. S., & Reinders, A. A. T. S. (2012). Fantasy proneness in dissociative identity disorder. Plos ONE 7(6) http://journals.plos.org/plosone/article?id=10.1371/journal.pone.0039279.

Norton, K. (1994). Inpatient psychotherapy at the Henderson hospital, In: V. Sinason (Ed.), *Treating Survivors of Satanist Abuse* (pp. 115–120). London: Routledge.

Ogawa, J. R., Stroufe, L. A., Weinfield, N. S., Carlson, E. A., & Egeland, B. (1997). Development and the fragmented self: longitudinal study of dissociative symptomology in a non-clinical sample. *Development and Psychopathology, 9*: 855–979.

Orbach, S. (1997). *The Impossibility of Sex*. London: Allen Lane.

Sachs, A. (2014, June). *Stable and Unstable DID*. Talk at Leipzig Trauma Centre.

Sachs, A., & Galton, G. (Eds.) (2008). *Forensic Aspects of Dissociative Identity Disorder*. London: Karnac.

Sinason, V. (Ed.) (1994). *Treating Survivors of Satanist Abuse*. London: Routledge.

Sinason, V. (1998). *Memory in Dispute*. London: Karnac.

Sinason, V. (2002). *Attachment, Trauma and Multiplicity: Working with Dissociative Identity Disorder*. London: Routledge.

Stobart, E. (2006). *Child abuse linked to accusations of "possession" and "witchcraft"*. Research report RR 750. Department for Education and Skills.

Tyrer, P. (2002). Nidotherapy: a new approach to the treatment of personality disorder. *Acta Psychiatrica Scandinavica, 105*: 469–471. PMID 12059852.

Van der Merwe, A., & Sinason, V. (2016). *Shattered but Unbroken: Voices of Triumph and Testimony*. London: Karnac.

Winnicott, D. W. (1973). *The Child, the Family and the Outside World*. London: Penguin.

Yalom, I. D., & Leszcz, M. (2005). *Theory and Practice of Group Psychotherapy*. New York: Basic.

FURTHER READING

Bromberg, P. (1998). *Standing between the Spaces*. Hillsdale, NJ: Analytic.

Cameron, D. E. (1956). Psychic driving. *American Journal of Psychiatry, 112*: 502–509.

Corbett, A. (2016). *Psychotherapy with Male Survivors of Sexual Abuse: The Invisible Men*. London: Karnac.

Delgado, J. M. R. (1971). *Physical Control of the Mind*. New York: Harper & Row.

Estabrooks, G. H. (1971). Hypnosis comes of age. *Science Digest*, April: 44–50.

Marks, J. (1988). *The Search for the Manchurian Candidate*. New York: Norton.

Milgram, S. (1974). *Obedience to Authority: an Experimental View*. London: HarperCollins.

Mollon, P. (2002). The dark dimensions of multiple personality. In: V. Sinason (Ed.), *Attachment, Trauma and Multiplicity: Working with Dissociative Identity Disorder* (Chapter 11). London: Routledge.

O'Brien, C., & Phillips, M. (1995). Trance Formation of America. http:// ia800306.us.archive.org/21/items/TranceformationOfAmerica/ tranceformation_america.pdf [last accessed 3 January 2017].

Oxnan, R. B. (2005). *A Fractured Mind: My Life with Multiple Personality Disorder*. New York: Hyperion.

Phillips, M., & O'Brien, C. (1993). Project Monarch Programming Definitions.

Rappaport, J. (1995). CIA experiments with mind control on children. *Perceptions*, Sept/Oct: 56.

Ross, C. A. (2000). *Bluebird: Deliberate creation of multiple personality by psychiatrists*. Richardson, TX: Manitou.

Segal, S. S. (1984). *Society and Mental Handicap: are we Ineducable?* Tunbridge Wells: Costello.

Sinason, V. (1986). Secondary mental handicap as a defence against trauma. *Psychoanalytic Psychotherapy, 2*: 2 (131–154).

Sinason, V. (1990). Passionate lethal attachments. *British Journal of Psychotherapy, 7*(1).

Sinason, V. (2002). Treating people with learning disability after physical or sexual abuse. *Advances in Psychiatric Treatment, 8*: 424–432.

Sinason, V. (2010). *Mental Handicap and the Human Condition*. London: Free Association.

Sinason, V. (2012). *Trauma, Dissociation and Multiplicity: Working on Identity and Selves*. London: Routledge.

Sinason, V., & Aduale, A. K. (2008). Safeguarding London Children.

Thomas, G. (1989). *Journey into Madness: the True Story of Secret CIA Mind Control and Medical Abuse*. New York: Bantam.

United Nations Treaty Series (1976). *International Covenant on Civil and Political Rights, 14668*(999): 171. https://treaties.un.org/doc/publication/unts/volume%20999/volume-999-i-14668-english.pdf [last accessed 3 January 2017].

Van der Hart, O., Nijenhuis, E. R. S., & Steele, K. (2009). *The Haunted Self: Structural Dissociation and the Treatment of Chronic Traumatization*. New York: Norton.

INDEX

105